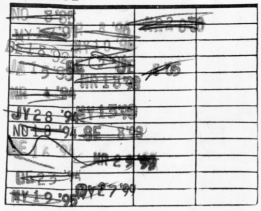

The
Jazz
Titans

A Da Capo Press Reprint Series

THE ROOTS OF JAZZ

General Editor: Christopher W. White

The Jazz Titans

INCLUDING "THE PARLANCE OF HIP"

by Robert George Reisner

DA CAPO PRESS • NEW YORK • 1977

Library of Congress Cataloging in Publication Data

Reisner, Robert George.
    The jazz titans, including "The parlance of hip".

    (Da Capo Press reprint series)
    Reprint of the 1960 ed. published by Doubleday,
Garden City, N.Y.
    1. Jazz musicians—Biography. 1. Jazz
music—Discography. I. Title.
[ML3561.J3R4 1977]   785.4'2'0924 [B] 76-58559
ISBN 0-306-70866-3

This Da Capo Press edition of *The Jazz Titans* is
an unabridged republication of the first edition
published in Garden City, New York in 1960.
It is reprinted with the permission of
Doubleday and Company, Inc.

Published by Da Capo Press, Inc.
A Subsidiary of Plenum Publishing Corporation
227 West 17th Street, New York, N. Y. 10011

THE JAZZ TITANS

Drawings by
Harrison Cruse

1960

The
Jazz
Titans

INCLUDING "THE PARLANCE OF HIP"

by Robert George Reisner

DOUBLEDAY & COMPANY, INC.

GARDEN CITY, NEW YORK

CONTENTS

THE TITANS

Don't tell me — I've left out Louis, Jelly
Roll, and Bessie. I'm sorry. I'm more ag-
grieved not to include Brew Moore, Allen
Eager, Zoot Sims, Benny Harris, George Wal-
lington, Al Haig, Kenny Dorham, Duke Jordan,
Lee Konitz, Dodo Marmarosa, Howard McGhee,
Oscar Peterson, Tadd Dameron, Tommy Potter,
Gene Ramey, Jimmy Raney, Curley Russell, Dex-
ter Gordon, the later Wardell Gray, Ernie Henry,
Serge Chaloff, and so many other beautiful modern
cats.

The titans have certain qualities in common; they
are all composers, they are all mold-breakers, they
are all major influences. Since I started writing the
book several have died. In many cases they died pre-
maturely, due in part to certain excesses of stimu-

lants. They are, nevertheless, martyrs to their art. Tremendous emotional strains bore down upon them as they strove to live with this vital expressive music. Great art calls for total involvement, which almost always means that the artist must have isolation. The jazzman creates constantly. He is not isolated even by stage distance. The audience is on top of him; drinking, talking, laughing, staring, judging, or critical. He must be cool or go mad. His special sense of integrity and personal pride make him want above all to please his peers, the guys on the stand. Their approval is his real applause.

I stand by my choices. I am suspicious of the beatniks, who dig everything. The hipster is selective. A short discography follows each profile, but it is safe to say that these musicians seldom cut a bad side. I came up through the ricky-ticky sound and the monotonous swing riff. If you missed them, there's always folk music and rock 'n' roll to graduate from. The jazz titans, those players of the gentle cool and the hard, funky bop, have given me tremendous joy. They'll knock you out too if you but open your emotions and receive their message. It is, essentially, love.

Bob Reisner

THE JAZZ TITANS

COUNT BASIE

The Friends of Basie Society a few years back held a testimonial dinner for him at the Waldorf-Astoria. There was a "This Is Your Life" guest list: Basie's proud father; his adopted father, John Hammond, who heard him over a small K.C. station in 1935 and has never stopped proselytizing; Willard Alexander, his manager; Pres (Lester Young), who flew in from Chicago; his old and new bands, and many other jazz luminaries.

Before he attained the title, just plain Bill struggled. In the summer of 1927 he hit Kansas City with a band led by a lady, Gonzelle White. The group folded, and Basie spent four months in a K.C. hospital with a nervous breakdown. It was probably the first and last rest he has ever had.

Leaving the hospital, he looked at the town and liked it. He found a job as organist at the Eblon movie house. He had learned the instrument from Fats Waller, who once held the same position at an uptown New York cinemateria. For two years Basie improvised appropriate music for Westerns, and then he left to join Walter Page's Blue Devils as pianist and arranger for a year.

Around 1932 he was in the Benny Moten band. In 1935, when Moten died, he formed his own nine-piece group and took it into the gangster-endowed Reno Club. They played seven nights a week from 10 P.M. to 5 A.M., including broadcasts and Sunday breakfast dances that lasted until nine or ten in the morning. Of their pay Basie has said: "Yeah, $2.50 a night. You were happy when you got one of those $4 gigs at a club."

The Count's personal life is devoid of eccentricities. He has a wife, daughter, dog, model trains, and eats up a storm. He conducts from the piano bench. Avoiding flourishes, he detonates his brilliant brass and horns with simple little phrases. He feeds just the right chords and riffs for the men to latch on to. His rhythm sections have always jumped steadily.

WHAT TO READ

Basie, William Count. In: Current Biography, 1942. Illus.

12

Hammond, John. "Twenty Years of Count Basie." In: Condon, Eddie, and Gehman, Richard, eds., Eddie Condon's Treasury of Jazz. New York, Dial Press, 1956. Pp. 250–257.

Horricks, Raymond. *Count Basie and His Orchestra.* New York, Citadel Press, 1957. Discography. Illus.

"Immortals of Jazz." *Down Beat.* June 15, 1941. P. 10.

Shapiro, Nat. "William 'Count' Basie." In: Shapiro, Nat, and Hentoff, Nat, *The Jazz Makers.* New York, Rinehart, 1957. Pp. 232–242. Discography. Illus.

WHAT TO HEAR

Basie.   Roulette R-52003.

Basie in London.   Verve MGV 8199.

Basie's Best.   American Recording Society G422.

Count Basie.   Norgran MGC-647.

Count Basie.   American Recording Society 401,402.

13

ART BLAKEY

"My father was a businessman. He hated jazz musicians." Art nevertheless studied piano in school. He was born in Pittsburgh, Pennsylvania, on October 11, 1919. He was playing professionally by 1936 with his eight-piece group at a place called the Democratic Club. The Democrats had pretty good taste, for they took Art away from the piano and told him to play the drums, putting a new man named Erroll Garner in his place. Blakey, without instruction, mastered the drums and developed an intricate and fiercely incisive style, passionate and unrelenting in its drive.

He married at fourteen. He believes that everyone should marry when his body and emotions are ready. Several years ago Blakey remarried. A recent arrival brings his total to four girls and a boy.

In 1939 he joined Fletcher Henderson's band. In

15

1940 he was with Mary Lou Williams' first group at Kelly's Stables. He then had his own band for a year at the Tic Toc Club in Boston, and 1944–47 found him with Billy Eckstine.

When that pioneer bop band folded, Art went traveling. He roamed through Nigeria, the Gold Coast, and India. He went to study Islam. His Mohammedan name is Abdullah Ibn Buhaina.

The travels added ideas to his drumming. In Africa the drummers hold their sticks in no set way except that which is most comfortable for them. Every man searches for his own sounds, makes his own music, creates his own style. Blakey is the most emotional and orgiastic drummer that has come upon the scene since Baby Dodds. Since 1953 he has headed his own group, the Jazz Messengers. Once in a while he changes personnel. He likes to give young cats a chance. When they can make the Blakey tempi, they can be sent out in the world to play with anyone.

Buhaina is always beating the drums musically and vocally for jazz. He makes ardent little speeches between sets: "What do the politicians want to send to Europe? Ballets! Symphonies! Why, man, that's where all that stuff came from! And here they want to send it back to 'em instead of sending something truly our own."

16

Frost, H. "Art Blakey in St. Louis." *Metronome*. February 1947. P. 26+. Illus.

Lovett, H. "Art Blakey." *Metronome*. June 1956. P. 17+. Illus.

Reisner, Robert. "Art Blakey: Jazz Messenger." *Nugget*. August 1959. Pp. 54–56. Illus. Discography.

Tynan, John. "The Jazz Message." *Down Beat*. October 17, 1957. P. 15. Illus.

Wilson, Russ. " 'Blues Are Basic,' Blakey Says." Oakland *Tribune*. July 7, 1957. P. B–15.

WHAT TO HEAR

Drum Suite.   Columbia. CL 1002.

Art Blakey and the Jazz Messengers.   Blue Note 4003.

A Night in Tunisia.   Vik LX 1115.

At the Café Bohemia. 2 Vols. Blue Note 1507/1508.

Jazz Messengers with Thelonious Monk.   Atlantic 1278.

17

JIMMY BLANTON

Bass solos can be a dull business. They often get a bigger hand because they are so tedious; people feel it's the thing to dig them. In the twenties and thirties bassists were left to play their one-three-five chords, thumping out the required number of beats to the measure and rarely soloing. Blanton changed all that.

In December 1939 this twenty-one year-old, slim, shy, quiet musician joined Duke Ellington's band at the Coronado Hotel in St. Louis. He was a student of Adolphus Alsbrook. His credits consisted of work in the bands of Jeter-Pillars and Fate Marable. He was a replacement for Billy Taylor (the bassist, not the pianist). Barry Ulanov phrased it adroitly when he wrote, "He took the bass out of the doghouse to which it had been traditionally assigned in jazz." "Doghouse" is the old slang term for the cumbersome instrument. Blanton pioneered a whole new concept. The beat became flowing instead of choppy, the syncopations more complex. He reached out to flatted fifths, ninths, thirteenths; his pizzicato and bow work gave the bass the solo qualities of a horn. Ellington featured him on records. "Jack The Bear" is considered one of the finest bass solos ever recorded. "Bear" became Blanton's nickname.

"Hey, Bear," a friend would say: "Some chick on the phone for you," and Blanton, absorbed in checkers, a pastime he loved almost as much as roller skating, would pick up the receiver twenty minutes later. He was a serious fellow. Mingus recalls that Lee Young, the drummer, and Joe Comfort, bassist, brought Bear around to hear Ming and cut him. "He had a warmth of tone I didn't have. He didn't play that night. He was too polite to be competitive."

Blanton was in the Ellington band for three years. "Plucked Again," "Pitter Panther Patter," "Jumpin' Punkins," and "Mr. J. B. Blues" are some of the discs which later influenced arrangers to write more harmonically important parts for the bass. A victim of congenital tuberculosis, Bear began to suffer from coughing spells. He was sent to a sanitorium in the hills of Los Angeles where he died a short while afterward, age twenty-four. Billy Strayhorn said, "Not only do the good die young; they suffer while they live."

WHAT TO READ

Emge, Charles. "Jimmy Blanton Takes Last Ride." *Down Beat.* August 15, 1942. P. 12.

Koonce, Dave. "Late Jimmy Blanton Bassdom's Greatest." *Metronome.* August 1946. Pp. 48–49.

Tanner, P. "Oh, Didn't They Ramble?" *Melody Maker.* August 12, 1950. P. 9.

WHAT TO HEAR

Duo. Duke Ellington-Jimmy Blanton.   Victor EP EPA-619.

Blanton replaced Taylor in October 1939. He can be heard on approximately thirty-five records until he was replaced by Junior Raglin in December 1941.

CLIFFORD BROWN

During a lashing rainstorm in June 1956, a car skidded on the Pennsylvania Turnpike and went over an embankment killing all the occupants: driver Nancy Powell, her husband, pianist Richie Powell; and Clifford Brown. They were on their way home to Philly. In 1950, Brownie had been in an auto accident that hospitalized him for a year. During the time Death deferred payment he made good the promise that his fellow musicians saw in him. Bird once said to Art Blakey as he was leaving town: "If you're going to Philadelphia, don't take a trumpet player with you."

Clifford Brown was born in Wilmington, Delaware, on October 30, 1930. None of the numerous instruments his father played interested him except the trumpet. When he entered high school he got one from his father as a gift. He studied harmony, theory, vibes, bass, and piano in addition to trumpet. Brown attended Delaware State, majoring in mathematics, and the next year switched to Maryland State College, studying music on a scholarship.

By May 1951 he had recovered from the first accident and played in a rhythm and blues outfit. The next year he was in the Hampton band, touring Europe. In 1954 he teamed with Max Roach, and in June of that year their quintet was presented at the Tiffany in L.A. The group clicked with the fans and clinked for the club owners.

His is a strong and fiery horn. There is sometimes the feeling of a race between his vivid imagination and the ability to cram those ideas into the space and time he has to say it in. The impress of Diz's and Fat's powerful resonances and of Miles's melodic fertility are heard in his nevertheless original style. He has written very lovely things, among them a piece dedicated to his wife, Larue. He lived to see the birth of his son. Wilmington set up a Clifford Brown Memorial Scholarship Fund. An eloquent composition, "I'll Remember Clifford" by Benny Golson with lyrics by Jon Hendricks, has been written in his memory. Among the many who remember him is Beverly Getz, wife of the great tenorman. When drugs took Getz's money and freedom for six months and she was with child, Brownie organized a benefit. He raised $350 for her. They had never met.

Butcher, M. "Clifford Brown; A Personal Tribute." *Jazz Journal.* August 1956. P. 1+. Illus.

Hentoff, Nat. "Clifford Brown — The New Dizzy." *Down Beat.* April 7, 1954. P. 15. Illus.

Hentoff, Nat. "Roach & Brown, Inc., Dealers in Jazz." *Down Beat.* May 4, 1955. Illus.

Jones, Quincy. "A Tribute to Brownie." *Down Beat.* August 22, 1946. P. 10+.

Morgan, A. "Talking of Fats and Brownie." *Melody Maker.* July 10, 1954. P. 9.

"Scholarship Fund Set Up to Honor Brownie's Memory." *Down Beat.* September 19, 1956. P. 19.

WHAT TO HEAR

At Basin Street.   Emarcy 36070.

Study in Brown.   Emarcy 36037.

Brown and Roach, Inc.   Emarcy 36008.

Clifford Brown Memorial.   Prestige 7055.

Memorial Album.   Blue Note 1526.

CHARLIE CHRISTIAN

Charlie Christian transformed the guitar in jazz from its plunk-plunk role to one of long solo flight. He amplified his instrument electrically and harmonically. For nearly twenty years guitarists have acknowledged their debt to a man whose entire professional life was less than half that long.

Born in Dallas in 1919, raised in Oklahoma City, he constructed homemade guitars out of cigar boxes when he was a child. A bit later, he was guiding his blind father, who was a guitarist and singer, from job to job. His first job for pay was at sixteen in a joint. He played bass for a while in Alphonso Trent's band, and then led his own combo.

His cultural inheritance was guitar country and squalor. No one knows where he got his stuff, but it is a safe assumption that a good deal of it came from

27

the fluidity and sinuousness of the Kansas City horns he heard playing the southwest territory. As Ralph Ellison says, "O.K. City was a stopping-off point for K.C. bands on the road and Lester Young's arrival 'with his battered horn upset the entire Negro section of town.' "

Christian's fame was local. Mary Lou Williams told John Hammond who told Benny Goodman. In the book *Jazz Makers*, Bill Simon tells how B.G., startled by the appearance of this "impossible rube" in a ten-gallon hat, yellow shoes, and green suit, did not give too attentive an ear during a short audition. But the same evening, with Christian on the bandstand, the surprised leader called for "Rose Room" and they jammed for forty-eight minutes.

Charlie Christian was a headliner for two years, appearing on virtually all the sextet records. He came up north to fame and with tuberculosis, which became critical. His life was furious. He'd play downtown with Goodman, then into a cab and uptown at Minton's; and in between he had a great, too great appreciation of the "chicks." To maintain the pace, or something, he smoked pot. Utterly bemused by the stuff, he listened one day to a friend relate a long tale of horrors committed by a fiend. Charlie nodded and said "Solid."

He was sent to a sanitarium on Staten Island. The doctors declared that he was making progress, but several of his new buddies kept sneaking him out for little "tea parties." During one, he contracted pneumonia. Christian died on March 2, 1942; age twenty-three.

WHAT TO READ

"Charlie Christian Dies in New York." *Down Beat.* March 15, 1942. Pp. 1, 20. Illus.

Ellison, Ralph. "The Charlie Christian Story." *Saturday Review.* May 17, 1958. Illus.

Simon, Bill. "Charlie Christian." In: Shapiro, Nat, and Hentoff, Nat, *The Jazz Makers.* New York, Rinehart, 1957. Pp. 316–331. Discography. Illus.

Stevens, A., and Giltrap, H. "Spare a Thought for a Jazzman of Yesterday." *Melody Maker.* April 19, 1952. P. 11.

Ulanov, Barry. "Hail! The Guitar." *Metronome.* November 1952. Pp. 14, 22. Illus.

WHAT TO HEAR

Benny Goodman Sextet & Orch. with Charlie Christian. Columbia CL 652.

The Harlem Jazz Scene — 1941.   Esoteric ES 548.

Benny Goodman Combos.   Columbia CL 500.

Benny Goodman Presents Fletcher Henderson Arrangements.   Columbia CL 524.

KENNY CLARKE

Klook, a name hung on him because it was the sound of a drum riff, lives in Paris and may never return. There, he says, he feels more like a man. Every critic and modern jazzman looks him up when in France. As for the sound, things could be better; French jazz is like American champagne.

Kenny Clarke studied piano, trombone, vibes, and theory. Born on January 9, 1914, in Pittsburgh, Pennsylvania, he started to play professionally at an early age. At twenty-one he was playing with Roy Eldridge. He did service in the bands of Leroy Bradley, Jeter-Pillars, and Edgar Hayes, making a European tour with the latter. He was with the Claude Hopkins band for eight months and then with Teddy Hill during 1939–40.

Clarke worked out interesting variations for drums

which gave him a real instrumental voice. In 1937 he began to change his style. With the right hand he rode the front cymbal, the focal point. With the left he added accents on the snare. The left foot took the high hat and the right foot dropped occasional "bombs" on the bass drum. He said that he had seen most drummers leave their left hand idle, and he had to find something to do with it.

When the Hill band broke up he took some of its experimentative members into Minton's. There the revolutionary clique of masters — Christian, Tadd Dameron, Thelonious, Diz, Bird, Powell — played their intricate music which, as Klook says, "kept the riffraff off the stand." Benny Goodman sat in with them one night, but they politely modified their style to fit his. Klook a bit later played with such traditionals as Armstrong, Red Allen, and Benny Carter. The Army gave him a gig in 1943, and he put on musical shows for them. When he returned to the States he went into Gillespie's band. In 1948 he hit the Old World for the third time. Touring North Africa, he was inspired to write "Algerian Cynicism" and to adopt a Mohammedan name, Liaqat Ali Salaam. He has written "Salt Peanuts" with Dizzy, "Epistrophy" with Monk, and "Mop Mop" with Ike Quebec. It is also a credit to his musical good taste that he was once married to Carmen McRae.

In 1952 he helped organize the Modern Jazz Quartet and stayed with the group until he developed a severe case of ennui. The doctor prescribed a more swinging climate.

WHAT TO READ

Clarke, Kenny. In: Shapiro, Nat, and Hentoff, Nat, *Hear Me Talkin' to Ya*. New York, Rinehart, 1955. Pp. 337, 339, 340, 342, 347–49, 349–50, 354, 391–2.

Hentoff, Nat. "The Modern Jazz Quartet." *High Fidelity*. March 1955. P. 38+.

WHAT TO HEAR

Klook's Clique.   Savoy MG 12065.

Kenny Clarke, Vol. 2.   Savoy MG 15053.

Kenny Clarke Plays Andre Hodeir   Epic LN 3376.

Strollin', Etc. Savoy 12006.

Kenny Clarke & Ernie Wilkins Septet. Savoy 12007.

MILES DAVIS

In Europe, Miles Davis is an idol. To his annoyance, they cheer even his mistakes.

Here his popularity reached a point where Columbia Records, a company not distinguished for "discoveries" in the jazz field, signed him up. In the early stages of his career he experienced difficulties with the fast upper-register work that some trumpeters tear your head off with. Since then he has mastered all the techniques, but in the process of compensating for his early deficiencies, he evolved his lyric, middle register, sometimes breathy tone. Lately it is his wont to fit a mute into a bell of his horn and stick it almost into the microphone.

He grew up in East St. Louis amid comfortable surroundings. His father, a dentist, gave him a trumpet and found him a teacher at thirteen. At fifteen he had a union card and was jobbing around. His first

35

favorite was Roy Eldridge, and later he and his friends strove to play in the style of Diz and Bird. In 1945, at nineteen, Miles came to New York and enrolled at the Juilliard School. He says: "I spent my first week in New York and my first month's allowance looking for Charlie Parker. I roomed with Charlie Parker for a year. I used to follow him around, down to Fifty-second Street where he used to play. 'Don't be afraid,' he used to tell me, 'go ahead and play.' Every night I'd write down chords I heard, on matchbox covers. Everybody helped me. Next day I'd play those chords all day in the practice room at Juilliard, instead of going to classes."

In September of 1948, Miles fronted a nine-piece band at the Royal Roost. The group laid a financial egg, but was an aesthetic giant step in jazz voicing, arrangement, and experimentation. Strongly influenced by Ellington and Debussy, eight beautiful originals were recorded by Capitol, 1949–50, and are available today.

Mercurial Miles, prince of cats in the night jazz world, is a cult leader without trying to be. Many of his followers delight in his unorthodoxies, wandering on and off the stand wearing extreme clothing, including the tightest pants in jazz. They match his tight trumpet. In the last four years he has become the most respected, recorded, recalcitrant, and "right" musician around. His popularity rated a female *Life* photographer, who, while setting up equipment and lights, said to him, "this may be an uncomfortable half hour, Mr. Davis."

Miles smiled bitterly and said, "It's all right lady. I've been uncomfortable for thirty-one years."

One evening I was sitting sadly in a club awaiting sidemen I had hired for a musicale. Davis walked in and sat patiently waiting with the rest of the clientele. The musicians finally arrived. Miles sat through a set, listening attentively, and then got up. On leaving, he said, "Man, give me $10." "Why?" I asked. He smiled. "For standing by."

WHAT TO READ

Anderson, J. Lee. "The Musings of Miles." *Saturday Review*. October 11, 1958. Pp. 58, 59, 66. Illus.

Burland, Sascha, and Reisner, Robert. "The Midnight Horn." *Nugget*. December 1958. Pp. 34, 35, 42, 64. Discography by Charles Edward Smith. Illus.

Hentoff, Nat. "An Afternoon with Miles Davis." *The Jazz Review*. December 1958. Pp. 9–12. Illus.

Hentoff, Nat. "Miles Davis: Last Trump." *Esquire*. March 1959. Pp. 88–90. Illus.

Hodeir, Andre. "Miles Davis and the Cool Tendency." In: *Jazz: Its Evolution and Essence*. New York, Grove Press, 1956. Pp. 116–36. Discography.

WHAT TO HEAR

Miles Davis, Vol. 1.   Blue Note 1501.

Miles Davis, Vol. 2.   Blue Note 1502.

Cookin' with the Miles Davis Quintet.   Prestige 7094.

'Round about Midnight.   Columbia 949.

Miles Ahead.   Columbia CL 1041.

Classics in Jazz Capitol.   H 459 (a ten-inch record).

BILLY ECKSTINE

Despite the fact that Billy Eckstine sometimes earns as much as a quarter of a million dollars a year and his fans number in
the tens of thousands, he can be a fine singer. He
was born William Clarence Eckstein in Pittsburgh,
Pennsylvania, July 8, 1914, and billed himself Xstine
until he finally came to be called "Mr. B." The "B"
could easily stand for bop, Eckstine's absorbing musical interest.

In 1944 he fronted a historic band which had
among its personnel Dizzy Gillespie, Charlie Parker,
Fats Navarro, Sonny Stitt, and Sarah Vaughan. B.
did vocals and played at trumpet and trombone. He
learned to sing by hanging around Washington, D.C.,
musicians (D.C. has produced some down cats), and
so he is not afraid to extend musical lines. His strong
voice belts, caresses, but never whimpers a lyric. A

39

lack of engagements and the recording ban finished the band in 1947. It was in hock to the tune of $19,000.

He went out as a single, doing club dates and during Easter of 1951 he got a call from the Copacabana. Sinatra had suffered a hemorrhage of the throat and was unable to make his midnight show. The Voice said that Mr. B. was the only singer in New York who could substitute. Eckstine was then playing the Paramount for the third time and had the management worried; dames were almost falling into the pit as he descended on the moving stage. Billy doubled that week, playing the Copa and the Paramount, and then collapsed from nervous exhaustion when it was over.

He's handsome, and after bop, clothing and golf are his main interests. He popularized the Slim Jim necktie and the roll shirt collar. His traveling retinue has included, on occasion, a golf pro. The scandal magazines have had their fun with him, talking out of the corner of their mouths about an alleged secret three-year affair with a model who bore him two children. Married in 1942, he broke amicably with his wife, June, eleven years later, at which time she said, "Let the poor boy live." And live he has. Denise Darcel, the French lady, is a fan. "Thees Beelleee," she said, "he ees a wondair."

Eckstine, Billy. In: Current Biography, 1952. Illus.

Eckstine, Billy. "Leading My Own Outfit." *Melody Maker*. August 28, 1954. P. 13. Illus.

"Mr. B." *Life*. April 24, 1950. Pp. 101–4. Illus.

Ulanov, Barry. "Mr. B." *Metronome*. July 1950. Pp. 13–14. Illus.

Vosburgh, D. "Mr. B Talks Shop." *Melody Maker*. June 4, 1955. P. 5. Illus.

WHAT TO HEAR

Billy Eckstine and His Orchestra. Recorded during years 1944–47, approximately 23 records on the Deluxe and National labels. All are 78s and not too easy to obtain.

Billy's Best. Mercury 20316.

Blues for Sale. Mercury 36029.

Eckstine's Imagination. Emarcy 36129.

That Old Feeling. MGM 3275.

DUKE ELLINGTON

The Duke received his title at age eight from a friend who was impressed with his impeccable dress. He owns more than one hundred suits, four hundred neckties. He is a gourmet and gourmand.

Composer-pianist-arranger-leader Edward Kennedy Ellington was born in Washington, D.C., on April 29, 1899. His career, in its fourth decade, is aesthetically and statistically breathtaking. Some eighteen million records have been sold. Collectors (the late King George V was one) have devoted years trying to complete an Ellington record collection. His first, "Jig Walk," was put out for use in nickelodeons in 1924. In the late twenties dime stores and newsstands carried one-sided paper-back records by his band. Including his first composition in 1915, "Soda Fountain Rag," and his latest, Othello-inspired "Such

43

Sweet Thunder," he has written fifteen hundred pieces.

He is genial, gallant, a hypochondriac, and cognizant of his genius. A magnificent mental balance keeps him always unruffled. This has enabled him to keep a band together over thirty years, constantly traveling and working.

Impressed by rent-party pianists like Lucky Roberts, Fats, and James P., the Duke began playing professionally at sixteen. In 1922 he made an unsuccessful attack on New York. He went home, but Waller talked him into another attempt. This time he made it. His group, The Washingtonians, played at Barron's and the Kentucky Club in Harlem. From 1927–32 he worked and built his reputation at the Cotton Club. Enamored of his music, the owners sent a hard boy to break Duke's contract with a Philadelphia theater. "Be big," said the gunman to Duke's manager, "Be big or be dead." The contract was broken.

Every ten years a story appears saying that the Duke is finished. He keeps right on writing shows, doing concerts, and crossing the pond to satisfy the Europeans, who have loved him since the days of his "jungle band." A recent discography by Benny Aasland lists 997 items, the last titled "Love You Madly," a favorite phrase of his. The distinctive, impressionistic Ellington style endures because personnel changes are few, considering the notable in-

44

stability of the business. The Duke writes with each man's musical inclinations in mind. He has been compared favorably with Delius. "Solitude" was written in twenty minutes, before a recording date.

Duke's music cannot be categorized in any of jazz's historical pigeonholes. It is hybrid. Duke says: "You need everything you can get. You need the conservatory — with an ear to what's happening in the street."

WHAT TO READ

Boyer, Richard O. "The Hot Bach." *The New Yorker.* June 24, July 1, July 8, 1944.

Clar, Mimi. "The Style of Duke Ellington." *The Jazz Review.* April 1959. Pp. 6–10. Discography. Illus.

Feather, Leonard. "Duke Ellington." In: Shapiro, Nat, and Hentoff, Nat, *The Jazz Makers.* New York, Rinehart, 1957. Pp. 187–201. Discography. Illus.

Gammond, Peter, ed. *Duke Ellington, His Life and Music.* London, Phoenix House, 1958. Discography. Illus.

Hobson, Wilder. "Duke Ellington." In: De Toledano, Ralph, *Frontiers of Jazz.* New York, Oliver Dur-

45

rell, 1947. Pp. 137–147. Reprinted from August 1933 *Fortune*. Illus.

Ulanov, Barry. *Duke Ellington*. New York, Creative Age Press, 1946. Discography. Illus.

WHAT TO HEAR

Early Ellington. Brunswick 54007.

Ellington Showcase. Capitol T 679.

The Music of Duke Ellington. Columbia CL 558.

Ellington Sidekicks. Epic LN 3237.

In a Mellotone. Victor LPM 1364.

ART FARMER

In the past few years Art Farmer has been
called in frequently on recording dates that
require accomplished musicianship. Elabo-
rate jazz scores demand a technician of Farmer's
abilities. If it were not for his steadfast devotion to
jazz, he might easily defect to the classical scene.
But, as he wryly says, "Jazz may become interesting
as an art, just as it is now an entertainment."

He came on the scene with his twin brother, bassist
Addison, on August 21, 1928, in Council Bluffs,
Iowa. Farmer started his musical education in public
school, going from violin to piano to bass tuba, de-
voting a year to each. In high school he settled on the
trumpet. He made his professional debut in L.A. in
1945 in the band of Horace Henderson. The Jay
McShann band took him in. They were once stranded
in Fort Worth, and Art told the boss he was hungry.

McShann took out seventeen cents, all he had, and offered it to him. Art graciously refused.

In the fall of 1946 he came to New York and took a job as a janitor. It was not the result of an aptitude test — but in order to study with Maurice Grupp, a teacher. Influenced by Navarro, Davis, Louis, Eldridge, H. Baker, Shavers, the late Freddie Webster (a legend among musicians), and Ben Bailey, Farmer nevertheless is very much Art Farmer. He has little trouble with identity. A person once asked how he could tell himself from his twin brother, and Art said, "That's easy. All I have to do is try to play bass."

He toured the continent with Lionel Hampton's band in 1953. "In Europe we started and we ended up with the bread-and-butter tunes. It was like a slice of bread on bottom and then some pretty nice fill-ins and then bread on the top." In March 1954 he began a successful collaboration with Gigi Gryce. His chart is jagged but always ascending. In a becalmed period he may have to do a commercial recording date. He emerged one day from a studio where he had just done a thing with strings. In the anteroom he saw some of his jazzmen friends. They told him they were there to do a date. He looked at them and asked, a little sadly, "Jazz?" Farmer is a trumpeter of taste, melodic fertility, and adaptive flexibility. He seemed quite at home in the Mulligan group as he is also in the less controlled combinations. He tells of an incident that happened while playing

48

with Gerry at Storyville. A young man came up to the stand as they were setting up. He asked Art for his autograph; Farmer wrote it out. The fellow read it, then turned to Mulligan and said, "Chet Baker not with you any more?"

Gerry said, "That's right." The cat tore up Art's autograph.

After listening to Farmer play one set, he came over and apologized for his brutal gesture.

"O.K.," Art said, "but don't tear up my replacement's autograph."

WHAT TO READ

Hentoff, Nat. "A New Jazz Corporation — Gryce, Farmer." *Down Beat.* October 19, 1955. Pp. 10–11. Illus.

Korall, Burt. "Art Is Farmer's Sake." *Metronome.* May 1957. Pp. 29, 37. Illus.

Wilson, John S. "Art Farmer" *The Collector's Jazz: Modern.* Philadelphia, J. B. Lippincott, 1959. Pp. 97–99.

The Art Farmer Quintet.   Prestige 12″ LP 7017.

Two Trumpets (with Donald Byrd).   Prestige 12″ LP 7062.

George Russell, the Jazz Workshop.   RCA Victor 12″ LPM-1372.

When Farmer Met Gryce.   Prestige 12″ LP 7085.

Portrait of Art Farmer.   Contemporary 12″ LP 3554.

Modern Art.   United Artists 12″ LP 4007.

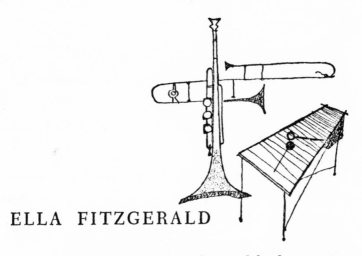

ELLA FITZGERALD

Ella was skinny and scared back in 1934, when at sixteen years of age she stepped out onto the stage of Harlem's Apollo Theatre. And well she might have been, for this was the Wednesday-night amateur show, prize $25 and a week's engagement. The audience was the hippest in the world, mostly Negroes. There were women in the crowd, maids and laundrywomen who sang at their work, most of which were better than Dinah Shore or Joni James or Kay Starr.

She had originally planned to dance, but something made her change her mind. Perhaps she glanced down at her spindly legs. She sang a tune called "Judy." The audience went wild, and she sang three encores and picked up the marbles.

A musician named Ali Bardu was fronting the band for drummer-leader Chick Webb that night.

He brought her before the maestro, and the famous association began. Webb and his wife took the girl from an orphanage into their home. On June 12, 1935, she made her first record with the Webb band: "Are You Here To Stay?"

The big one was written by Ella and recorded on May 2, 1938: "A-Tisket A-Tasket." It became a national hit, and after a while a drag on Ella when requested. In 1939, Webb died and she fronted the band for three years. In 1946 she summed up calypso before it all began with "Stone Cold Dead in the Market."

Among the pros she has always been, in the words of Bing Crosby, "the most." For twenty-three years Ella has been growing larger and larger in the public's estimation. She's also been growing in stage presence — that is, putting on weight. The increase is in the tradition of many female singers: Bessie Smith, Mildred Bailey, Sarah Vaughan, Billie Holiday, Chris Connor, etc.

Decca and Victor never did showcase her to full advantage. Only in the past few years has she been making albums full of solid tunes with full-bodied orchestras backing her clear tones, flexible range, and strong rythmic momentum (for example, Verve MG-4001-2).

Born April 25, 1918, in Newport News, Virginia, she was married (1948–52) to Ray Brown. She also tried movie-making, a silly little short years ago and a magnificent few episodes in *Pete Kelly's Blues*.

WHAT TO READ

"Apollo's Girl." *Time*. April 3, 1950. Pp. 70–71. Illus.

"Ella Fitzgerald: Her Vocal Versatility Continues to Amaze Musicians." *Ebony*. May 1949. Pp. 45–46. Illus.

Feather, Leonard. "Ella Meets the Duke." *Playboy*. November 1957. Illus.

Fitzgerald, Ella. In: Current Biography, 1956. Illus.

Simon, George T. "Ella Fitzgerald." *Metronome*. April 1950. Pp. 13–14. Illus.

WHAT TO HEAR

Like Someone in Love.　Verve 4004.

Lullabies of Birdland.　Decca 8149.

Sings the Cole Porter Song Book.　2 records. Verve 4001–2.

Sweet and Hot.   Decca 8155.

Ella — Songs in a Mellow Mood.   Decca 8068.

STAN GETZ

When most kids were thinking about the big game Saturday or a date for the movies and a Chinese dinner, Stan Getz was playing horn with Jack Teagarden. Big T. had to take out guardianship papers to keep Getz out of the truant officer's grasp. Before that he had played weddings in the Bronx when he was twelve and was with Richard Himber at fourteen. He quit school at fifteen and joined Dick "Stinky" Rogers' band, but the authorities caught him and threw him back to his classes.

Born in Philadelphia on February 2, 1927, Stan was not too young to handle a horn on Fifty-second Street in the late forties. It was a tender age to have to cope with night life, liquor, fast ladies, and the evil pills and powders proffered by friends. After a short interlude with Dixieland, which he graciously describes as a "foundation," he moved into music. (He also said about Dixie: "It's simple enough, but their jazz ideas are out of the question.") Using a light "cool" tone, inspired by Lester Young, he became a most moving balladeer. What he lacked in sonority he more than compensated for in momentum. He is capable of stomping when he chooses, but more often his inate musical refinement leads him into the gentler paths. On some records, as with Johnny Smith, a quiet guitarist, Smith takes the first quarter of the side and Getz comes in ever so gently, as if afraid to intrude.

Getz is like Mr. Memory in *The 39 Steps*. He remembers every number in the book of every band he played in. (His first wife, a singer, ruefully remarked, "I think the only reason he married me was that I could teach him a lot of tunes.") He was with Bob Chester, Kenton, Randy Brooks, Buddy Morrow, Jimmy Dorsey, B.G., and Herman. It was with Herman that he made "Early Autumn." Do not be disillusioned, but the solo in that piece was completely written out by Ralph Burns.

Considering the hectic professional life he has crammed into thirty-three years, it is a wonder that he has time for trouble, but he manages. In 1954 a drug habit (he threw it off) got him in a panic and he attempted to rob a drugstore, using his hand to simulate a gun. He fled when his bluff was called. Conscience-stricken, he called, apologized to the proprietor, and was arrested. Supporting a father, family, and a seventy-dollar-a-day habit became too much, and he attempted suicide in his cell. That failed also. He was shown clemency and reciprocated by straightening out completely. His influence on European jazz is marked. He now lives in Denmark. Sweden is not the same after his visits. He has a reputation as a tireless jammer, going from club to club, staying longest at Nalen, a night spot he particularly likes.

WHAT TO READ

Frost, H. "Two Sides of Stan Getz." *Metronome.* July 1957. Pp. 12–13. Illus.

Gleason, Ralph J. "Perspectives." *Down Beat.* September 5, 1956. P. 26.

Hentoff, Nat. " 'I Have the Right Band Attitude Now,' says Getz." *Down Beat.* March 9, 1955. P. 2. Illus.

Tynan, John. "Meet Dr. Getz." *Down Beat.* February 20, 1957. P. 13+. Illus.

Ulanov, Barry. "The Sound: Stan Getz, That Is, and That's Cool Jazz." *Metronome.* June 1950. Pp. 13–14. Illus.

The Stan Getz Quintet at Storyville. Vol. 1. Roost 2209.

The Sound. Roost 2207.

Moonlight in Vermont. Roost 2211.

At the Opera House. Verve 8265.

Stan Getz Quartets. Prestige 7002.

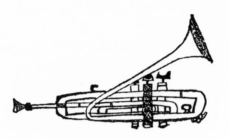

DIZZY GILLESPIE

John Gillespie appeared for his first professional job in Philadelphia. He was seventeen years old and too poor to afford a case, so he carried his trumpet in a paper bag. One of the musicians looked at the paper bag and said: "What a dizzy guy."

Going backward, he had studied at the Laurinburg Institute in North Carolina at fifteen. He played the trombone when he was fourteen. At three years of age he toddled over to the piano and "just picked it up."

Diz was born in Cheraw, South Carolina, on October 21, 1917. Before he started to front his own bands he put in apprenticeships with Edgar Hayes, Cab Calloway (whose coattails he once cut in antic humor), Benny Carter, Charlie Barnet, Les Hite, Earl Hines, Duke Ellington, and Billy Eckstine.

His great dancing — he sometimes leads his band

with his hips — is only equaled by his comedy, which is surpassed in turn by his brilliance as an instrumentalist. Like all of the titans, he has composed several staple tunes — "Woodyn You," for example, and "Night in Tunisia." He is a good cook and a formidable chess player.

A natural clown, he enjoys saying to the audience, "I'd like to introduce the members of the band." Then he introduces the musicians, one by one, to each other.

No stranger in Paris and London, Birks, as his close friends call him — that's his middle name — has been ambassadoring for the United States in such distant places as Abadan, Karachi, and Dakar.

Besides the amazing triple-tongue runs, the effortless changes, the bebop phrases, the clear melodic sense which can all be heard on the approximately 175 records he has cut, there are the physical trademarks concocted by Gillespie's intellectual, high-spirited temperament: bop glasses, goatee, beret, meerschaum pipe, easy laugh, S-shaped stance, and bent trumpet.

He lives on the same block as Louis Armstrong in Corona, Long Island, in a comfortable home. It's a coincidence of some sort, because Dizzy has been the greatest single trumpet influence to date since Satch.

Boyer, Richard O. "Bop: A Profile of Dizzy." In: Condon, Eddie, and Gehman, Richard, eds., *Eddie Condon's Treasury of Jazz*. New York, Dial Press, 1956. Pp. 206–21. Reprinted from *The New Yorker*. 1948.

Feather, Leonard. Inside Be-bop. New York, J. J. Robbins, 1949. 103 pp. Discography. Illus.

Feather, Leonard. "John 'Dizzy' Gillespie." In: Shapiro, Nat, and Hentoff, Nat, *The Jazz Makers*. New York, Rinehart, 1957. Pp. 332–47. Discography. Illus.

Gillespie, Dizzy. In: Current Biography, 1957. Illus.

McKean, Gilbert S. "The Diz and the Bebop." In: Gleason, Ralph J., *Jam Session*. New York, Putnam, 1958. Pp. 148–56. Reprinted from *Esquire*, October 1947.

Reddick, L. D. "Dizzy Gillespie in Atlanta." *Phylon*. Vol. 10, pp. 44–49, 1949.

WHAT TO HEAR

Dizzier and Dizzier.   RCA Victor LJM-1009.

61

Jazz Creations.   American Recording Society G-405.

World Statesman.   Verve 8174.

The Champ.   Savoy 12047.

Manteca.   Verve 8208.

GIGI GRYCE

Armed with a metal clarinet and a repertoire consisting of the *William Tell* Over-
ture and "Poet and Peasant" which he
played by ear, Gigi decided to get in on high school
functions. This was in Hartford, Connecticut, where
he was raised. He was born in Pensacola, Florida,
November 28, 1927. His primary goal was medicine.

After finishing high school he did a stint in the
Navy around the mid-forties. With shipmates like
Clark Terry, Jimmy Nottingham, and Willie Smith,
he turned irrevocably to music. Gryce got himself
thoroughly schooled on both sides of the musical fence
and has emerged as one of the important arrangers,
composers, and instrumentalists in jazz. On the classi-

cal side was study under Alan Hovhannes at the Boston Conservatory; Nadia Boulanger and Arthur Honegger in Paris (as a Fulbright scholar). On the jazz side there were three fellows he met in the Navy in North Carolina. They took command of his pay and made him buy an alto. They were Andrew "Goon" Gardner, alto, an authority on ideas; Julius Pogue, tenor, an authority on changes; and Harry Curtis, an authority on the technique of the alto. These people, plus twenty exercise books, were his training. He also studied flute and piano.

Jobbing around the Hartford area he began to make a name for himself among the people with ears. The payments and the spacings of these dates were so sparse that Gigi was literally starving. He had become thin as his reed. Someone had let him stay in a cold-water flat in Boston. There was nothing in the icebox but music manuscripts. One day he lay across the bed just waiting for his death and putting down his feelings in a tone poem, "Gashiya," Arabic for the overwhelming event. He kept his door open so that someone would find him if he passed out. A neighbor put a little food in him. Things began to change. He got to Paris on a scholarship, came home, and worked with Max Roach and Howard McGhee in New York. He joined Lionel Hampton's band and recrossed the pond. In the band was Art Farmer, with whom he teamed up. Their association established both men in the wider jazz world. Gigi has composed dozens of beautiful compositions, e.g., "Wildwood," "Hymn to The Orient," but he remembers his first with most amusement. It was called "Atomic Bounce."

WHAT TO READ

"Caught in the Act." *Down Beat*. May 2, 1956. P. 8.

"Gryce and Sims." *Down Beat*. January 1947. P. 36.

Hentoff, Nat. "A New Jazz Corporation — Gryce, Farmer." *Down Beat*. October 19, 1955. Pp. 10–11. Illus.

Horricks, Raymond. "Three Pied Pipers." *Jazz Journal*. January 1955. P. 3.

Nevard, M. "A Guy Named Gryce." *Melody Maker*. November 28, 1953. P. 7. Illus.

WHAT TO HEAR

Gigi Gryce.   Signal S 1201.

Jazz Lab.   Columbia CL-998.

Jazz Lab Quintet.   Riverside 12-229.

65

When Farmer Met Gryce. Prestige 7085.

Art Farmer Quintet Featuring Gigi Gryce. Prestige
7017.

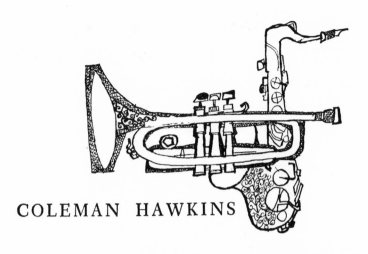

COLEMAN HAWKINS

On his ninth birthday Hawk got a tenor. At twelve he had a mustache and was playing commercially. Some say he invented the instrument, but he laughs and speaks of such jazzmen as Happy Cauldwell and Stomp Evans, whom he heard in Chicago and K.C. For thirty-five years he has played and progressed. "Where there's good musicians, you'll always find me." That's his credo.

He was an early admirer of Diz and Bird and assembled a group for a first bop session in February 1944. He has always played modern, whether it was with Mamie Smith's Jazz Hounds in 1922 or Thelonious Monk in 1960. Ten years with Fletcher Henderson established his reputation as *the* bad man on horn. After the regular job on the Roseland bandstand where Smack's (Henderson's) band was a regular, Coleman would get calls to make a session.

"Hawk," a voice would say, "you've got to cut this smart cat," and he would be off to do battle with Chu Berry, Prince Robinson, or Bud Freeman, boys, he said, who "tried to catch me on my bad nights."

A trip to Canada gave him a taste of the Old World, and one evening he got European eyes. He sent a wire to Jack Hylton, a prominent British bandleader. This was six years before he cut "Body and Soul" (1939), but they knew him. In a few days he was on the *Ile de France.* He told Fletcher that it was a two months' sabbatical, but he stayed in Europe more than six years, playing with every conceivable group. The most fantastic gig he recalls was in France with a hundred-piece symphony orchestra. "I was the only jazz thing on the program, doing one number, 'Talk of the Town,' in B natural. There was an opera singer and a cello soloist."

Hawk's tone is lush and heavy, but this tendency toward the syrupy is offset by its buoyancy. He came home in 1939 to find that nothing was happening musically. "They were laying for me. They thought I would be stale after six years in Europe. This was the real chance to catch me. They always wanted to cut me, why me? They had nothing new. At first I thought they were holding back, but it was not so. This'll be no strain." It was not until the advent of the cool school that something new was said and Hawk was there, listening and, now and then, learning.

68

Feather, Leonard. "Coleman Hawkins." In: Shapiro, Nat, and Hentoff, Nat, *The Jazz Makers*. New York, Rinehart, 1957. Pp. 163–174. Discography. Illus.

"Immortals of Jazz, Coleman Hawkins." *Down Beat*. February 15, 1940. P. 18. Illus.

Levin, Michael. "Coleman Hawkins One of the Great Forces in Jazz." *Down Beat*. October 20, 1950. Pp. 2–3.

Lim, Harry. "Hawk!" *Metronome*. May 1944. P. 16. Illus.

Stewart-Baxter, D. "Coleman Hawkins." *Jazz Journal*. October 1956. P. 3. Illus.

WHAT TO HEAR

Hawk in Hi-Fi.   Victor LPM 1281.

Hawk Talks.   Decca 8127.

The Hawk Flies High.   Riverside RLP 12-233.

Coleman Hawkins and His All-Stars.   Concert Hall CHJ 1201.

Monk's Music.   Thelonious Monk Septet with Coleman Hawkins. Riverside RLP 12-242.

Coleman Hawkins: A Documentary. 2 records. Riverside 12-117/18. No music. Hawk chats on a variety of subjects.

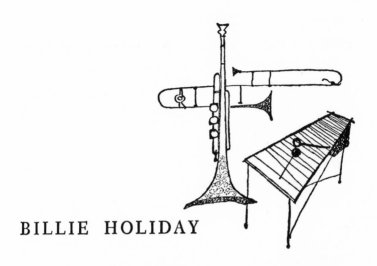

BILLIE HOLIDAY

Lady Day became a professional sufferer. She told of her woes on records, in night clubs, in a book, in the press, and in magazines. It all made for juicy copy. E.g., "How I Blew a Million Dollars," "Can a Dope Addict Come Back?", "I'm Cured for Good Now."

She and her art overcame a horrendous childhood: separated parents, rape, a foster home, tattered clothes, and hunger.

She was an existentialist singer because her songs were her. In the lyrics she appealed to all the injustice-collectors of the world: "Gloomy Sunday" (a tune forbidden in Budapest because people were committing suicide to it), "Loveless Love," "Good Morning, Heartache," "Billie's Blues," and "Don't Explain," a song she wrote when she found another woman's lipstick on one of her innumerable husbands. Her adult life was a seesaw of big money and crooked managers, concerts and cures, divorces and *Down Beat* awards.

At fourteen she got her first start in music. "One day we were so hungry we could hardly breathe" [her mother and herself in New York]. I started out the door. I walked down Seventh Avenue, going in every joint trying to find work." She found it in a place called the Log Cabin. She said at first she was a dancer, but the bluff failed. Billie then said she sang, and proved it by reducing the customers to limp rags. It did not take the musical VIPs long to realize that here was the greatest expressionist jazz singer since Bessie Smith.

She made her first record with Benny Goodman in 1933. Two musicians who helped by their exquisite taste were Teddy Wilson, pianist on so many early records, and Pres. Her grief at the death of Lester Young must have been profound. "I used to love to have him come around and blow pretty solos behind me." They were once in love — and they died in the same year.

The past few years Billie made a strong comeback. Her performances at times were uneven, just barely sustained by mannerism and myth, but she always made the lyric believable. The 1956 and '57 jazz-records reviews of *Down Beat* gave five stars to six of her albums of those years, the highest rating it bestows.

72

This lovely artist died Friday, July 17, 1959, at the age of forty-four. At her bedside was William Dufty, a close friend and her biographer, who has written accounts in the New York *Post* of her harassment by the police. She had a record, one on which she never sang. Years ago the insane were treated as public spectacles; today it is the addict.

WHAT TO READ

Bellerby, V. "The Art of Holiday." *Melody Maker*. February 27, 1954. P. 12. Illus.

Holiday, Billie. "I'm Cured for Good." *Ebony*. July 1949. Pp. 26–32. Illus.

Holiday, Billie, with William Dufty. *Lady Sings the Blues*. New York, Doubleday, 1956. Discography. Illus.

Keepnews, Orrin. "Lady Day Returns." *Record Changer*. June 1948. Pp. 8–9. Illus.

Smith, Charles Edward. "Billie Holiday." In: Shapiro, Nat, and Hentoff, Nat, *The Jazz Makers*. New York, Rinehart, 1957. Pp. 276–95. Discography. Illus.

Billie Holiday.   Commodore 30008.

Lady Day.   Columbia Cl-637.

Body and Soul.   Verve 8197.

Lover Man.   Decca 8702.

Lady in Satin.   Columbia CL-1157.

MILT JACKSON

M.J.Q. stands for Milt Jackson Quartet.
This is not meant to minimize the talents
of the other members of the Modern Jazz
Quartet, but it was Milt who kept his group together
during the lean years before December 1952 when
they made their big success with sides like "Vendome"
and "La Ronde." Whatever town the quartet played,
Milt's first stop was at a place where he bought pots
and pans to feed them. He cooks superbly (pineapple
pies are his specialty).

He was born in Detroit and attended Michigan
State. Dizzy was casting around for sideman to ac-
company him in a concert there. He used Jackson,
who knew the bop repertoire. Milt was doing amazing
things on what has been described as a "real torn up
one-and-a-half-octave set of vibes held together with
rubber bands and chewing gum." Dizzy brought him

to New York. That was in 1945. He composed, arranged, doubled on piano and guitar, and even sang on occasion. He did dates with Howard McGhee, Monk, and was in the Woody Herman band (1949–50). He was a sixth of the famous sextet with Gillespie, Parker, Ray Brown, Stan Levey, and Al Haig.

He started late in life, musically, "taking up the piano" at the age of eleven. He went on to study voice and harmony, singing with gospel groups in Detroit. Two versions suggest how he drew the nickname Bags. One is that his suits always hung loosely on his trim frame; and the other is that late hours put bags under his eyes.

When he settled on the vibraharp there were only two strong men, Lionel Hampton and Red Norvo. Bags soon established his pre-eminence. He is an artist of consummate taste and sensitivity with a tendency to say a little less and tell a lot more. His playing is characterized by a wistful lyricism over an underlying strength. He has a tantalizing sense of time. He will lag just a bit behind the beat, toying with it (as does Erroll Garner). He is pensive, profound, and poetic.

The M.J.Q.'s rise was meteoric, but their star seems fixed. The group has come in for its share of criticism. The school of hard swingers has dubbed them "The Undertakers" because of their conservative clothes and jazz. Their original drummer, Kenny Clarke, cut out for France and has said, "Milt Jackson is a great

76

jazzman whose hands are tied in this group; he'll wind up by quitting too." But M.J.Q. has done fine things for jazz. They gave emphasis to the elements of arrangement and composition. They on occasion give Bags a chance to "stretch out" especially on the blues he loves. One night he played so much that Percy Heath (bass) shook his head mournfully. "Bags is weeping all over the place," he said.

WHAT TO READ

Goodwin, K. "Milton 'Bags' Jackson." *Jazz Journal.* July 1957. P. 7. Illus.

Hentoff, Nat. "The Modern Jazz Quartet." *High Fidelity.* March 1955. P. 38.

Morgenstern, D. "Bags Groove." *Down Beat.* November 27, 1958. P. 17+.

"Recording Artists' Roster," *Down Beat.* June 30, 1954. P. 107.

WHAT TO HEAR

Plenty, Plenty Soul.   Atlantic 1269.

The Jazz Skyline.   Savoy 12070.

Jackson'sville.   Savoy 12080.

Django.   Prestige 7057.

Modern Jazz Quartet.   Prestige 7059.

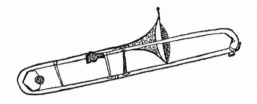

J. J. JOHNSON

The school band in Crispus Attucks High School, Indianapolis, in 1937 had everything but a trombone player when J. J. applied, so he took it up to be with his friends. After graduation he did post-graduate work on the road with a territorial band led by one Snookum Russell. In this band was a fellow of lively spirits, given to roughhouse but showing great promise. He inspired J.J. His name was Fats Navarro, and he died ten years later, but not before he became the Young Man with a Horn of the bop era.

J.J. stayed with the band for a year and a half, until the bookings became slack and the group evaporated. Then J.J. sadly returned to his parents. He was quickly hired by Benny Carter. After B.C. came C.B. — Count Basie.

While he was playing with the Count, he became

79

aware of the new movement in jazz. In his words: "It captured me completely, right off the bat. So different from what I had heard, but so right, I wanted to be in on it. Only thing was to listen to them play. First thing that came to my attention was the fact the harmony was more substantial. Altered chords and more chords and added related chords." J.J. listened. He now plays with a dexterity that confounds. He sounds like a valve trombone.

There were a couple of years, 1952–54, when "things began getting sort of wound up" — disappointments, hang-ups — so he left the jazz scene. Not many people in the Sperry factory knew that one of their blueprint inspectors was one of the greatest jazzmen.

By spring of 1954 he returned to music and teamed up with another noted trombonist, Kai Winding, to form the Jay and Kai combo. They toured and recorded successfully for two years without ever locking horns.

J.J. or Jay Jay, who is James Louis Johnson, born January 22, 1924, got his sobriquet by modestly signing all his arrangements "J.J." He is married to a girl from his home town and is twice a father.

"Caught in the Act." *Down Beat.* November 28, 1956. P. 10.

Coss, Bill. "Johnson and Kai Winding." *Metronome.* April 1955. P. 24.

Goodwin, K. "J.J. Johnson." *Jazz Journal.* February 1956. P. 9. Illus.

Hawker, Mike. "I Don't Recognize Hot, Cool and Bop." *Melody Maker.* September 7, 1957. P. 9. Illus.

Stewart-Baxter, D. "The Trombone." *Jazz Journal.* March 1956. Pp. 4–5.

WHAT TO HEAR

Dial J.J. 5.   Columbia CL-1084.

J.J. Johnson, Vol. 3.   Blue Note LP 5070.

Jay and Kai Quintet.   Prestige 7030.

The Eminent Jay Jay Johnson. 2 Vols.   Blue Note 1505, 1506.

J.J. Johnson and Kai Winding: Trombone for Two. Columbia CL 742.

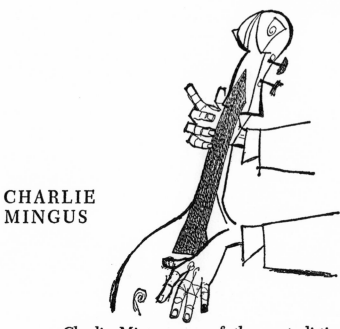

CHARLIE
MINGUS

Charlie Mingus, one of the most distinguished and creative bassists in jazz, has tough fingers and a tough uncompromising nature. Like the Bird, no one messes with the man or his music.

For his fingers he occasionally uses oil of turpentine. In his youth he made friends with the trombone, the piano, which he still plays on occasion, and the cello, which he exchanged for the bass when he got bigger. He believes in a fair fight.

Mingus followed Jimmy Blanton in elevating the bass to the status of a solo instrument rather than just a rhythmic accompaniment to horns blowing solos.

He composes constantly on and off the stand, and his music is more highly arranged than in most small groups. It is absorbing to watch him talking it up, exhorting his group, singing to them the lines he is composing while playing. "Work, work!" he will shout affectionately as a soloist extends a solo line into strange chordal territory.

Charlie Mingus was born in Nogales, Arizona, in 1922, and since 1940 he has played with such diversified groups as Kid Ory's, Alvino Ray's, and Art Tatum's. He has toured extensively, won polls, cut great sides such as the "Jazz at Massey Hall" series and "Phithecanthropus Erectus."

For the past few years he has been a conversational storm center. He is outspoken. Jazz to Mingus is a serious and dignified business which brooks no gimmicks and clowning. When I asked him when the big thing started happening for him in jazz, he said: "Never." A good part of the "never" referred to the precarious economics of the musician. "The only people associated with jazz that are making the money are the cats who are writing about it." He went on with good-humored irony: "I had a job with the post office not too long ago, but this security was taken from me by Charlie Parker, who called me up, reminded me of my aesthetic responsibilities, and made me give up my chance at a pension and Blue Cross. I joined his group and took the roller-coaster life of the jazzman."

84

Balliett, Whitney. "Mingus Blows Hot." *The New Yorker*. November 9, 1957. Pp. 115–18.

"Charlie Mingus." *Down Beat*. January 11, 1956. P. 18.

Gleason, Ralph J. "Charlie Mingus: A Thinking Musician." *Down Beat*. June 1, 1951. Illus.

Hentoff, Nat. "Mingus in Job Dilemma, Vows 'No Compromise.'" *Down Beat*. May 6, 1953. Illus.

Ulanov, Barry. *Down Beat*. October 3, 1956. P. 16.

WHAT TO HEAR

Jazzical Moods.   Period SPL 1107.

Mingus at the Bohemia.   Debut DEB-123.

Pithecanthropus Erectus.   Atlantic 1237.

Mingus Three.   Jubilee JLP 1054.

The Clown.   Atlantic LP 1260.

Mingus Ah Um.   Columbia CS 8171.

THELONIOUS MONK

When the teacher — hero of *The Black-board Jungle* — tells off one of his pupils and wants to impress him with his (the teacher's) hipness, he mentions the name of Theloni-ous Sphere Monk. In Thurston Scott's book, *I'll Get Mine,* the hero likes to listen to a record of Monk playing his composition, *Epistrophy*. In an expensive French magazine — *Cahiers d'Art,* No. 2, 1949 — I saw a painting by Victor Brauner, a noted surrealist, entitled "Thelonius." These are a few examples of how novelists and artists have played press agent to Monk. Eleven years ago a major story appeared in *PM* (see bibliography) which described him as a complete weirdo, and so the legend started.

He is a main cog among the cognoscenti, but the mystery surrounding him, the stories, the seeming unorthodoxies have tended to obfuscate his solid accomplishments. Monk is one of the pioneers of modern jazz, a pianist of tremendous technique and originality. His runs, broken rhythms, brave new chords, tone clusters, and time sense make listening an experience. He is the composer of over fifty tunes, a great many of which are part of the standard repertoire of contemporary jazzmen. The most familiar of these compositions is "Round About Midnight," perhaps the most beautiful jazz melody in the world.

Monk has a sly and sharp put-down sense of humor. Once on a radio appearance, a well-meaning interviewer said: "Mr. Monk, is it true that when you play certain augmented fifths juxtaposed by diminished sevenths you achieve particular dissonances and atonalities?" There were a few seconds of silence and then Monk said, in a slow drawl: "I try to play pretty." On another occasion, asked why he plays such strange chords, he said, "Those easy chords ain't so easy to find now." These self-minimizing and sardonic remarks do not reflect Monk's genuine feelings. He is uncompromising and sure about his music. While others were reaping financial rewards, Monk went his way, knowing that time would catch up with him.

He was born in New York City on October 10, 1920. His father was named Thelonious and Monk's son is named Thelonious. He wears a beret and various other caps because they are "handy" (he can put them in his pocket). He wears a goatee and on him it looks good. The dark glasses are prescription and tinted slightly to offset glare. He is a well-built man of regal bearing. Monk's originality so delighted many cats that they began to imitate his dress, hence the name "monkeys." The surface may seem bizarre, but when one gets close to the man and his music there is nothing but rationality and brilliance.

WHAT TO READ

Bacon, Paul. "The High Priest of Be-Bop: The Inimitable Mr. Monk." *Record Changer*. November 1949. Pp. 9–11, 26.

Brown, Frank London. "Thelonious Monk." *Down Beat*. October 30, 1958. Pp. 13–16, 45, 46. Illus.

James, Michael. "Thelonious Monk — a Personal Appreciation." *Jazz Monthly*. July 1957. Pp. 8–9. Illus.

Peck, Ira. "The Piano Man Who Dug Be-Bop." *PM*. February 22, 1948. Illus.

Smith, Charles Edward. "The Mad Monk." *Nugget*. October 1958. Pp. 52–53, 68, 70. Discography. Illus.

Genius of Modern Music. Vol. 1.   Blue Note 1510.

Genius of Modern Music. Vol. 2.   Blue Note 1511.

Brilliant Corners.   Riverside 12-226.

Thelonious Monk.   Prestige 7027.

Thelonious Monk.   Prestige 7075.

GERRY MULLIGAN

In 1952, Mulligan came up with what everyone was searching for — a new sound.

He formed his pianoless quartet and within two years achieved international success. In 1954 he played Paris and took the town. The French at that time were Crow Jim, believing that only American Negro musicians with French names like Louis and Bechet could play jazz.

Mulligan's music is characterized by clarity, restraint, and taste; it is, in a word — cool. He says, "I consider the string bass to be the basis of the sound of the group, the main thread around which the two horns weave their contrapuntal interplay."

Born in New York City and raised in Philly, he made his early reputation as an arranger and composer. If he does nothing else his contributions to the Miles Davis 1949 Capitol date will keep him in the books. For that session he wrote "Jeru," "Venus de Milo," and "Rocker." He worked for and in the bands of Gene Krupa, Elliott Lawrence, and Claude Thornhill. All this experience on the East Coast does not prevent his being pegged a West Coaster. All his initial publicity came from the Black Hawk in San Francisco and The Haig in L.A. It was there that audiences were treated to fugal versions of "My Funny Valentine," "Frenesi," "Turnstile," and other Fantasy and Pacific Jazz sides. They were also told to shut up or get out when their talk bugged the counterpoint.

At Newport he gets the biggest hand of all, and it is not just the music. His appeal to the more literate musical teen-ager and collegians is considerable. It is identification. There is a cool-cat, James Dean quality about him, a curious blend of formality and mock formality. Here, one feels, is a rebellious, restless nature yet harnessed to a severe art form, through a difficult instrument that when played poorly sounds like a big kazoo.

Leaving the park after a concert, he is jostled by two guys. Gerry sticks his thumbs in his belt, glowers at them, and invites them to rumble. He accompanies this with the promise that he will kick their teeth in. They cool it. A few hours later Mulligan is the aristocrat, sipping a cocktail in the home of the Lorillards. He is now ready to jam all night.

WHAT TO READ

Coulter, Glenn E. "Gerry Mulligan." *Cambridge Review*, No. 5. March 1956. Pp. 122–31.

Hentoff, Nat. "In the Mainstream." *The New Yorker*. March 21 and 28, 1959.

James, Michael. "Gerry Mulligan." *Jazz Monthly*. November and December 1957 (two parts). Illus.

Mulligan, Gerry. "The Importance of Jazz Tradition." *Down Beat*. September 21, 1955. P. 14+. Illus.

Tracy, Jack. "Says Gerry Mulligan, 'Get rid of the amateurs.'" *Down Beat*. July 25, 1956. P. 13. Illus.

WHAT TO HEAR

Gerry Mulligan Quartet.   Pacific Jazz 1207.

Paris Concert.   World Pacific 1210.

The Gerry Mulligan Sextet.   Emarcy 36056.

Mainstream.   Emarcy 36101.

The Gerry Mulligan Quartet.   World Pacific 1228.

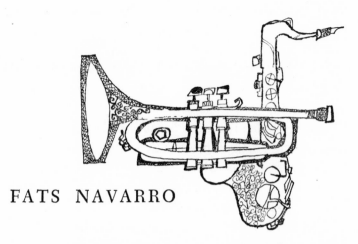

FATS NAVARRO

Theodore Navarro was one of the inspirations in the bebop (a word he didn't like) movement. "It's just modern music, it needs to be explained right, it's really a series of chord progressions."

His father was a hairdresser and part-time musician. Navarro got piano lessons at six, trumpet lessons at thirteen, and tenor-sax tutoring at sixteen. He left his home town of Key West (a place he didn't like) at eighteen and toured. He did two-year stretches with Snookum Russell, Andy Kirk, and Billy Eckstine. Howard McGhee, a trumpeter in the Kirk band, was an influence. Earlier inspirations were Roy Eldridge and Charlie Shavers, his third cousin. Navarro's trumpet was clean, fast, warm, and technically perfect. In 1946 he was an indefatigable free-lancer who could be heard in Minton's and on Fifty-second Street.

He began to get offers. Benny Goodman, seeing the course of history, was trying to bop in December 1947. Fats made one side with the sextet ("Stealin' Apples"). Duke Ellington made him an offer, but the salary was too low. Navarro, a gentle and soft-spoken person, said, "Dad, the sound would knock me out, but I can't make it on the bread." At about this time he acquired a drug habit that in a few short years was to aggravate a tubercular condition and kill him.

He took a job with Lionel Hampton, who offered him money to take Kenny Dorham's place. Hamp may have paid Fats a good salary to tweak Dorham. Fats has been described as one of the most literally unselfish guys who ever lived. He shared whatever was on his person. If he ate a sandwich, the person with him got half. He must have been racked by terrible inner churnings; they allowed him only twenty-seven years of life. Nothing in his outgoing manner indicated this. He was glib and gentle and was sometimes kiddingly called Fat Girl. He was playful and mild-mannered except on rare occasions. On one job there was a band bully. He went so far as to try to impress the others with a gun. He tried this caper with Fats, who with trumpet speed disarmed him, straddled the fellow, and held a jagged Coke bottle against his throat. "I'm sorry, baby," Fats murmured sweetly, "but I've gotta cut you just a little bit to show you I'm not kidding."

"Fats Navarro Dies in NYC." *Down Beat.* August 11, 1950. P. 1.

Morgan, A. "Talking of Fats and Brownie." *Melody Maker.* July 10, 1954. P. 9.

Simon, George T. "Fats Navarro." *Metronome.* October 1950. P. 13.

Ulanov, Barry. "Fats Navarro." *Metronome.* November 1947. Pp. 19, 38, 39. Illus.

Woodfin, H. A. "In Memoriam: Fats Navarro." *Saturday Review.* March 14, 1959. Pp. 71, 77. Illus.

WHAT TO HEAR

The Fabulous Fats Navarro. 2 Vols. Blue Note 1531, 1532.

Bud, Klook, Sonny, Kinney. Savoy 12011.

New Sounds in Modern Music. Vol. 1. Savoy 9005 (10 inch).

Modern Jazz Trumpets. Prestige 113 (10 inch).

Nostalgia. 2 Vols. Savoy MG 12138.

CHARLIE PARKER

They called him Bird because he was free and he sang. He was a legend even before his death in 1955. He seemed to have sprung full-blowing from nowhere, and yet his early life reveals an environment that was all music. As a boy of twelve he hung around in the alleys, putting his ear to the back doors of clubs like the Reno and the High Hat, hearing the fine Kansas City jazz. A few years later he had his horn.

A high school teacher named Efferge Ware taught him the rudiments. He played sessions and came in for his share of criticism. He began to woodshed (go off by oneself and practice) in earnest. It is said that no one ever passed the Parker home without hearing the sound of his alto. One of the great tragic-hero figures of the twentieth century, he was hooked onto the main power line of life. In his thirty-four years (sixty-eight when you consider he never slept) he was, as the French say, completely engagé. He was married at fifteen and acquired three other wives at various times. Asked his religion, he described himself as a devout musician.

Getting off a freight train, he landed in Chicago looking like a tramp, walked into a club, borrowed a horn for a set, and astounded every musician in the place. From then on he seemed to turn up everywhere, even as far out as Canada. In 1939 he was a dishwasher in New York. In 1947 he returned from a breakdown in California to conquer Fifty-second Street.

The speed of his playing was the first thing that got to people. Slow down these records to 16 r.p.m. and you hear perfect little structures. His authority, direct attack, and lyric fierceness have never been surpassed. He is to jazz what Picasso is to art. Bird is a major god of the Beat Generation because he dug everything and every scene. He could be found chatting with workmen in the Ukrainian section of New York where he lived or panhandling on the Bowery. Charlie Parker died in the home of his friend the Baroness de Koenigswater.

A Negro genius, he lived in a schizophrenic world of rejection and adulation. His influence dominates small-combo jazz and has filtered into Hollywood big-band arrangements. As they wrote crudely in chalk all

100

over sidewalks and subways a few days after his death, "BIRD LIVES."

Born August 29, 1920, in Kansas City, Kansas, and died March 12, 1955, New York City. Played clarinet and baritone horn in the school band. Shortly afterward his mother bought him an alto saxophone. He left the Lincoln High School in K.C., Missouri, in his third year. He was fifteen when he played his first professional job. In K.C. he played in the bands of Lawrence Keyes, Harlan Leonard, and Jay McShann. With the latter he made his first records in 1940. He did a nine-month stint with Noble Sissle's band, and in early 1942 he joined Earl Hines. In 1943 he played club dates with small groups and in 1944 made several sides for Savoy Records. In August 1946 he suffered a nervous breakdown in California but recovered after six months. He returned to New York in 1947 and came into full recognition as one of the leading exponents of modern jazz. He was a consistent winner of *Down Beat* and *Metronome* awards. In 1949 he played at the Jazz Festival in Paris. In the 1950s he commanded $1000 a date. In his last years he worked sporadically because of illness. A heart seizure was the last word except for the music, and, as the chalk said: Bird lives.

Coss, Bill. "Charlie Parker." Metronome Yearbook 1956. Illus.

Feather, Leonard. "Bird." Condon, Eddie, and Gehman, Richard, eds., *Eddie Condon's Treasury of Jazz*. New York, Dial Press, 1956. Pp. 228–36.

Gehman, Richard, and Reisner, Robert George. "Bird." *Playboy*. January 1957. Pp. 37, 38, 46, 52, 76. Illus.

Hodeir, André. "Charlie Parker and the Bop Movement" In: *Jazz: Its Evolution and Essence*. New York, Grove Press, 1956. Pp. 99–115. Discography.

Keepnews, Orrin. "Charlie Parker." Shapiro, Nat, and Hentoff, Nat, *The Jazz Makers*. New York, Rinehart, 1957. Pp. 202–17. Discography. Illus.

Reisner, Robert George. "Bird." Condon, Eddie, and Gehman, Richard, eds., *Eddie Condon's Treasury of Jazz*. New York, Dial Press, 1956. Pp. 236–41.

Charlie Parker. 4 Vols.   Dial 201-203, 207.

The Genius of Charlie Parker. 8 Vols.   Verve MGC 5003, MGV 8004-8014.

The Charlie Parker Story.   Savoy MG 12079.

Charlie Parker Memorial. 2 Vols. Savoy MG-12000, MG-12009.

The Magnificent Charlie Parker.   Clef MGC-646.

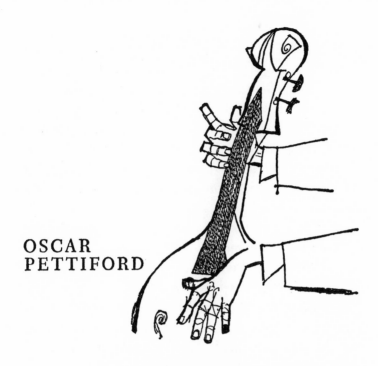

OSCAR
PETTIFORD

Oscar Pettiford, world-renowned bassist, came to New York with the Charlie Barnet band in 1943. That same year he left the band to form his own group, a quintet composed of Diz (who became co-leader), Don Byas, George Wallington, and Max Roach. They were, historically, the first bop band on Fifty-second Street, playing the Onyx Club for four months.

The next year Pettiford won first place in the *Esquire* and *Metronome* polls. In 1954 he married. Things were happening. He spent two and a half years with the Duke, and has been the heartbeat of many a great group.

O.P. is original. He composes: "Bohemia After Dark," "The Gentle Art of Love," and "Swingin' Till the Girls Come Home" are but a few. He once wrote, in admiration of Mitropoulos, "Beat Me, Dimitri." He is inventive. The five-stringed bass was his idea. He successfully adapted his bass style to an amplified cello, an instrument on which he performs beautifully.

Pettiford was born on an Indian reservation in Okmulgee, Oklahoma, in 1922. He was one of thirteen children, all of whom were musicians. His father, Harry "Doc" Pettiford, was the leader of one of the best jazz bands in the southwest territory. Mother was a music teacher, and at one time eleven Pettifords were in the band. Shades of Johann Sebastian.

"I got started at six years old. I used to dance with my father's band. When I was seventeen I had a short role with Olsen and Johnson in Minneapolis. Before I settled on the bass I played piano, trombone, trumpet, which hurt my jaws, and I studied tailoring in case the music business ever got too tough."

His chronicle includes a peripatetic education in eight states. In Minnesota several superior basketball players allowed him in a game. They beat him, nudged his ribs, tripped him, and infuriated him to the point where he challenged all five to a fight. The superior team went back to the clubhouse with various abrasions. When the story came to light it was doubly embarrassing, because the players were Golden Glove contenders. Oscar was persuaded to enter. He did and won the Minneapolis Golden Gloves. "But five guys?" I asked. "Weren't you scared?" He gave a big smile and said: "I figured they'd get in each other's way."

In 1958 he was involved in the number-one killer of titans, a car accident but has since fully recovered.

WHAT TO READ

"An Oscar." *Down Beat*. March 21, 1957. Pp. 17–18. Illus.

Harris, Pat. "Oscar Pettiford Now on Cello Kick." *Down Beat*. December 29, 1950. P. 20. Illus.

"Heard in Person." *Down Beat*. May 16, 1957. Pp. 33–34. Illus.

Mitchell, Bruce. "An Oscar for Oscar." *Esquire*. September 1957. Pp. 106–8. Illus.

"Oscar Pettiford." *Metronome*. May 1957. P. 30+. Illus.

O.P.'s Jazz Men.   ABC Paramount 227.

Oscar Pettiford.   Bethlehem LP BCP 1003.

Another One.   Bethlehem 33.

Oscar Pettiford Orchestra in Hi-Fi.   ABC Paramount LP 135.

Oscar Pettiford Orchestra in Hi-Fi. Vol. 2.   ABC Paramount LP 227.

BUD POWELL

Musicians say of pianist Earl "Bud" Powell that "he's somethin' else," in the sense that he's in a class by himself. A native of New York City, he was born September 27, 1924. His father was a professional pianist, a brother played trumpet, and another brother, Richie, was a fine jazz pianist who was tragically killed in an automobile accident a few years ago.

Bud began his formal training at the age of six. For seven years he played the masters. Popular music began to absorb him, and at fifteen he left school to wander amid the jungle night spots of Coney Island. Slowly, he worked his way uptown, stopping off as solo pianist for a while in Greenwich Village at a place called The Place (now The Limelight).

He worked in Cootie Williams' band in 1943–44, and after that he was a familiar figure on The Street

(Fifty-second) and uptown at Minton's, where he "chewed up" every pianist in sight. Even his idol Art Tatum found him a phenomenon. His lyric speed, his appoggiaturas and bravuras gassed Tatum as they do everyone when Bud is "on." Tatum once had his chauffeur drive Bud home in his Cadillac — for Art, the ultimate compliment.

In 1945 he began to be plagued by feelings of paranoia and suffered a series of nervous breakdowns that were to keep him in and out of mental institutions. As his reputation grew, he received better treatment during his periods of confinement. Gone were the dousings with ammoniated water, and the beatings. His recoveries have always been rapid, and the present prognosis is good.

Music is so much his life that once when a friend visited him in a hospital, Bud sketched the piano keys on the wall. Banging his fingers against it, he said: "Listen, what do you think of these chords?"

WHAT TO READ

"Jazzman's jazzman." *Newsweek.* September 10, 1956. P. 96. Illus.

Mehegan, John. "The New Pianism." *Down Beat.* June 27, 1956. P. 13.

Morgan, A. "The Bud Powell Trio." *Jazz Journal.* April 1954. P. 3. Illus.

Morrison, Allan. "Can a Musician Return from the Brink of Insanity?" *Ebony.* August 1953. Pp. 67, 68, 70–74. Illus.

Pease, Sharon A. "Bud Powell's Unique Style Has Widespread Influence." *Down Beat.* June 15, 1951. P. 16. Illus.

WHAT TO HEAR

The Amazing Bud Powell. 2 Vols.   Blue Note 1503, 1904.

Bud!   Blue Note 1571.

Piano Interpretations.   Norgran LP MGN-1077.

The Genius of Bud Powell.   Verve 8115.

Bud.   Roost 2224.

MAX ROACH

In modern jazz every session is a trial of manhood. Max Roach developed his speed, technical precision, and variety of beats in the early grueling, night-after-all-night bop sessions at Minton's and Clarke Monroe's Uptown House. He played with Dizzy Gillespie and Charlie Parker, who set such fast tempos that he had to develop patterns beyond the straight four-to-the-bar rhythm. He appeared in a solo in the movie *Carmen Jones*, and it would not have been a mistake to make him the lead, for he is lean, hard, handsome, and six feet tall.

To watch Max work is to see a man calmly beating the hell out of various drums, paying special attention to the cymbals to get a legato feeling, rather than the old heavy bass-drum sound. He beats up those drums unmercifully, graduating tones to such a fine degree that I have "heard" him execute a few strokes upon

113

the air at the end of a solo. He leaves audiences collapsed, and a master of ceremonies once called his group "Murderers' Row," after the Yankee line-up.

Max was born in Brooklyn on October 1, 1925. For fourteen years he has been playing professionally. That means he has coolly sweated over the drums about five thousand times, a tenth of which would wreck the average man. Drummers are a hardy group. Krupa is pushing fifty. Tony Sparbaro, a member of the Original Dixieland Band (1914–25), is still playing. Kenny Clarke, whom Max cites as an important influence, is playing in France.

Max is a consistent poll winner. Year after year he trades top places with Art Blakey, Jo Jones, Buddy Rich, and, on occasion, Clarke. But he always wins, places, or shows.

WHAT TO READ

Feather, Leonard. "Facts about Max." *Metronome*. November 1948. Illus.

Gold, Don. "Max Roach." *Down Beat*. March 20, 1958. Pp. 15–16.

Harris, Pat. "Stravinsky, Bird, Vibes Gas Roach." *Down Beat*. June 3, 1949. Illus.

Hentoff, Nat. "Roach & Brown, Inc., Dealers in Jazz." *Down Beat.* May 4, 1955. Illus.

Moscrop, J. "Why We Began to Play." *Melody Maker.* January 27, 1951. P. 8. Illus.

WHAT TO HEAR

Max Roach Plus Four.   EmArcy MG 36098.

Jazz in 3/4 Time.   EmArcy MG 36108.

Clifford Brown and Max Roach at Basin Street.   EmArcy 36070.

Jazz at Massey Hall. 2 Vols.   Debut 2/3 (10 inch).

Charlie Parker All Star Sextet.   Roost LP 2210.

SONNY ROLLINS

In the last few years the most influential and original tenor has been Sonny Rollins.

His absorption and ingestion of the masters Hawkins, Young, and Bird led to his own forceful, driving, hard bop style which in turn has influenced a bevy of young tenormen; Griffin, Mobley, Urso, Rouse, and Coltrane. A thoughtful experimenter, he is reaching farther and farther out in the long improvised solo. At times he eschews the use of the rhythm section. He does incredible things with the corniest tunes, Broadway or pop stuff like "Surrey with the Fringe on Top," "How Are Things in Glocca Morra?", or "I'm an Old Cow Hand."

He feels he may have been recording before he was ready. The first date was at 18 with Babs Gonzales for Capitol, in 1948. There was always the sound of some kind of music in his house. An older brother was of concert-stage caliber on the violin but turned to medicine. Sonny studied piano at nine and in high school began playing alto. He later attended the New York School of Music. In 1955 he went west to cerebrate at the University of Chicago. He worked at the Beehive and for a time gigged as a day laborer.

A large person, he bears a striking resemblance to Don Newcombe and when in beard looks like he could play Othello. Musician and musicologist Gunther Schuller says, "Rollins can honk, blurt, cajole, scoop, shrill — whatever the phrase demands without succumbing to the vulgar or obnoxious." Until recently he has been a sort of underground musician. The subterraneans dug him years ago for his work with Miles, Bud, and Thelonious. The *nouveau hip* discovered him when he made beautiful unison things with Max Roach and Clifford Brown. In between, during what may be called an eclipse of the Sonny, a guitar-player friend took him to the Catskills and he played a few hotels in the borsht circuit. They loved him and some seasons later when Rollins was big and the guitar player returned to Fallsburgh alone, the nice customers kept asking, "Vere's Sonny? Vat heppened to Sonny?"

Balliett, Whitney. "Jazz Records." *The New Yorker.*
June 15, 1957. P. 78.

Cerulli, Dom. "Theodore Walter Rollins." *Down
Beat.* July 10, 1958. Pp. 16–17. Illus.

Hadlock, Dick. "Sonny Rollins' Freedom Suite." *The
Jazz Review.* May 1959. Pp. 10–11. Illus.

Hentoff, Nat. "Sonny Rollins." *Down Beat.* November 28, 1956. Pp. 15–16. Illus.

Schuller, Gunther. "Sonny Rollins and the Challenge
of Thematic Improvisation." *The Jazz Review.*
November 1958. Pp. 21, 69. Illus.

WHAT TO HEAR

Saxophone Colossus.   Prestige LP 7079.

Sonny Rollins. 2 Vols.   Blue Note 1542, 1558.

Sonny Rollins Plus 4.   Prestige 7038.

Way Out West.   Contemporary C 3530.

Freedom Suite.   Riverside 12-258.

HORACE SILVER

The word most often used to describe the playing of Horace Silver is "funky." This term, which originally meant a pungent odor, has come to mean, in music, earthy and fundamental. Horace plays fundamental piano that is highly percussive. For a time he was called "Señor Blues" because of a best-selling record and also because of his preoccupation with the blues form. He gets a lot of gospel, African call and response in his amen music. His ferocious drive and hunched concentration have rounded his shoulders slightly. He moves, and those on the stand cook along with him.

Silver was born in Norwalk, Connecticut, on September 2, 1928. This makes him a Virgo, the title of one of his compositions. I hold no brief for horoscopy but studs under this sign are: hard workers, a bit nervous (see *Parlance*), given to artistic work.

In all of his albums the majority of the compositions are Silver originals. Teddy Wilson and Art Tatum influenced him. Bud Powell jolted him. He was playing tenor sax and piano in Hartford. Getz heard him, and he became part of Stan's quintet (naturally he did not play tenor) for a year, 1950–51. Blue Note picked him up early; they recently awarded him a silver record for ten years of outstanding performance on their label. He has the reputation among fans, musicians, and employers of having an affable and amiable disposition. Nothing bugs him except: night clubs with badly tuned pianos; bad mikes; club managers who have switched policies, know nothing of jazz, and treat musicians "like you worked in the kitchen."

Virgos, it is said, are critical and analytical. This fits Horace. "The youngsters who dig the faggot-type groups may grow up to play like that. I hope they dig more of the right things, the masters like Bird, Bud, Tatum, Lester Young, Coleman Hawkins, Miles, Sonny Rollins — the guys with depth." Title-givers who use his surname in every obvious *double-entendre* may well dub his next album "Hi Yo, Silver."

WHAT TO READ

Balliett, Whitney. "Jazz Records." *The New Yorker.* October 26, 1957. Pp. 174–76.

122

Feather, Leonard. "Pieces for Silver." *Down Beat.* August 22, 1957. P. 31. Illus.

Hentoff, Nat. "Even Mynheers Turn to Silver." *Down Beat.* October 31, 1956. Pp. 17–18. Illus.

Kopel, Guy. "Horace Silver et les 'Prêcheurs.'" *Jazz Magazine* (Paris). April 1959. Pp. 22–27. Illus.

Wilton, John S. "Horace Silver" *The Collector's Jazz Modern.* Philadelphia, J. B. Lippincott, 1959. Pp. 271–72.

WHAT TO HEAR

Blowin' the Blues Away.   Blue Note 12" LP 4017.

Finger Poppin'.   Blue Note 12" LP 4008.

Further Explorations.   Blue Note 12" LP 1589.

Horace Silver & The Jazz Messengers.   Blue Note 12" LP 1518.

Horace Silver Trio with Art Blakey.   Blue Note 12" LP 1520.

Six Pieces of Silver.   Blue Note 12" LP 1539.

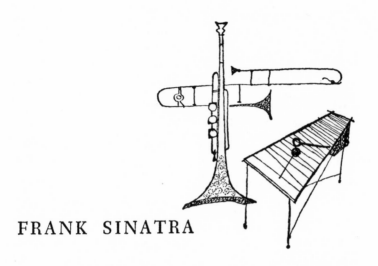

FRANK SINATRA

The Voice is in the enviable position of being both a popular idol and a musician's singer. He makes it for everyone from bobby-soxer to intellectual. To get an understanding of Sinatra's widespread appeal is to realize that he is a microcosm of the American character. He embodies, in one set of cells, furious energy, ambition, sentimentality, violence, and fair play.

Here is the rags-to-riches story of a boy who was doing eighteen shows a week for carfare and rose to the point where a TV network invested $3 million in him. Here is dynamism that subsists on three or four hours' sleep a night. Here is our dark and secret Warner Bros.-instilled admiration for hard guys.

Frank's interest in pugilists reflects our latent violence. His grandiloquent gestures, like singing directly to a young child in the audience, or working for scale for a night club owner's widow, are an American characteristic. They spring from the same schmaltzy urge which causes national concern over the elopement of an heiress and a pauper.

Even scrapes with the press and his unco-operativeness (he is one of those rare people who hires a publicity agent at $30,000 a year to shoo off reporters and writers) present him as a Goliath facing a David. Through all his fights there runs a strong vein of the fair-play element: his fight to keep his private life his own; his battles for racial justice and equality; his taking up the cudgels for ASCAP against BMI in an attempt to get good music on the radio; his defense of the Hollywood Ten, a cause in which he was enlisted by his friend Bogart; his devotion to Roosevelt and Stevenson.

When we come to Sinatra the musician, tantrums and quirks fall away and all we have is the consummate artist, a singer who has the field to himself. He came up when Bing was starting on his decline. He started a trend which gave emphasis to male vocalists, but all seem to have melted from the scene — except those who have turned part comedian. Discounting publicity flukes, gimmick singers, and "wholesome" types, the only male singers who sing with rich sensuality are Joe Williams and Billy Eckstine (watch also old time newcomer David Allen).

Sinatra does all his recording in the evenings, between eight and twelve midnight. He allows a studio

126

audience. They really have to be fans, for he will do as many as twenty-one takes before he gets what he wants. "Yeah, yeah, I think that's the one. Whadda you think?"

WHAT TO READ

Davidson, Bill. "Life Story of Frank Sinatra." *Look.* May 14, May 28, June 11, 1957. Illus.

Kahn, E. J. Jr. *The Voice.* New York, Harper, 1947. Illus.

Pryor, T. M. "Rise, Fall and Rise of Sinatra." New York *Times* Magazine Section. February 10, 1957. Pp. 17+. Illus.

Reisner, Robert George. "Sinatra." *Playboy.* November 1958. Pp. 62–64, 66, 84–88. Illus.

Sinatra, Frank. Current Biography, 1943. Illus.

WHAT TO HEAR

Only the Lonely.   Capitol W-1053.

Songs for Swingin' Lovers.   Capitol W-653.

Wee Small Hours.　Capitol W-581.

Where Are You?　Capitol W-855.

Close to You.　Capitol W-789.

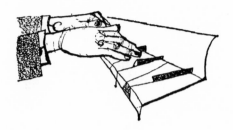

ART TATUM

Well-grounded in classical music, Tatum would read scores, a magnifying glass against his one functioning eye, which gave him only 25 per cent vision. Rachmaninoff said: "Had Tatum not preferred syncopation to the classics, he might have become the world's greatest pianist."

He did become one of the greatest jazzmen, his style florid and dazzling. He played with incredible speed, changing tempos, keys, and mood. He veered from fluid runs to the "stride" style of Walter and James P.

Starting on violin, at thirteen, he switched to piano at fourteen. In Toledo, Ohio, where he was born on October 13, 1910, there is a sign on the door of one O. J. Ramey which states that he was the teacher of Art.

In a few years he was staff pianist for radio station WSPD. He stayed at this job three years, simultaneously playing local night clubs in Toledo and Cleveland. In 1932 he got a position as accompanist to singer Adelaide Hall. During one show Miss Hall was changing costumes and Art had the audience to himself. He couldn't resist, and he unleashed some dying arpeggios. The applause was such that Tatum had to finish the show. That same year he took his own trio into New York's Onyx Club.

In the thirties he was pre-eminent, mostly because of constant club work rather than recordings. It was twenty years before he was archivized, and then Norman Granz in 1954 did it with a vengeance: two hundred piano solos on eleven twelve-inch discs entitled "The Genius of Art Tatum."

In 1943 with Tiny Grimes, guitar, and Slam Stewart, bass, he commanded the highest price for a trio on Fifty-second Street. The Three Deuces paid him $1000 a week. Spotting Art in the audience where he was playing, Fats Waller proclaimed: "God is in the house tonight." When asked to name his own favorite three piano deities, Tatum said: "Horowitz, Horowitz, Horowitz."

He was to appear on a Steve Allen Sunday TV show on November 11, 1956, but he passed away suddenly on November 6. He was the last of the great after-hours or back-room musicians. A guy who warmed at the prospect of a "cutting" session, he once "carved" a fellow pianist in a promethean twenty-four-hour piano duel.

WHAT TO READ

Balliett, Whitney. "Art, and Tatum." *Saturday Review*. October 29, 1955. P. 44. Illus.

Hodeir, André. "Art Tatum." *Down Beat*. August 10, 1955. Pp. 9–10, 12. Illus.

Hodeir, André. "Critic's Reply to Billy Taylor." *Down Beat*. November 2, 1955. P. 34. Illus.

Keepnews, Orrin. "Art Tatum." Shapiro, Nat, and Hentoff, Nat, *The Jazz Makers*. New York, Rinehart, 1957. Pp. 151–162. Illus. Discography.

Pease, Sharon A. "Tatum's Genius Sparks Modern Dance Rhythm." *Down Beat*. July 1, 1944. P. 12. Illus.

"Solo man." *Time*. December 5, 1949. Pp. 56–58. Illus.

Taylor, Billy. "Billy Taylor Replies to Art Tatum Critic." *Down Beat*. September 21, 1955. P. 17. Illus.

The Genius of Art Tatum. 11 Vols.   Verve.

Here's Art Tatum.   Brunswick 54004.

Presenting the Art Tatum Trio.   Verve MG V-8118.

Art Tatum-Roy Eldridge.   Clef 679.

LENNIE TRISTANO

If, as Marx said, "struggle is happiness," then pianist Lennie Tristano should be deliriously happy. This Schönberg or Einstein of jazz, as he's been variously called, has struggled. In 1946, when modern jazz was fighting for acceptability, he cut historic sides for Keynote Records. Another session with Capitol Records in 1949 further fortified the case for bebop.

These records have not lost one jot of freshness to this day. Some of the titles are "I Can't Get Started," "Atonement," and "Cooling Off with Ulanov" (a critic who consistently championed Tristano).

The pianist was born in Chicago on March 19, 1919. At six a case of measles weakened his eyes. A few years later he was blind. He entered a state institution in Chicago where he stayed from age nine to nineteen. Under a set of rigorous rules, this place lumped every type of individual together, brilliant or feeble-minded. Lennie said: "It either made an idiot of you or a person."

Tristano availed himself of the advantages. He studied piano, saxophone, clarinet, and cello. He formed his own band and they were allowed off grounds to play local taverns in town. He next attended a conservatory where he skipped off with a Bachelor of Music degree in three years.

In 1946 he came to New York. For the next five years he was a familiar figure playing all the clubs and gathering a coterie of disciples around him. Lennie's brilliant extensions of jazz harmonies made him a leader and a teacher. His most famous pupil is Lee Konitz, but even musicians of such disparate styles as Bud Freeman and Bob Wilbur have been to the maestro's studio.

Lennie's public appearances are rare. He says: "I have found great degrees of hostility in the music business. It is a grueling profession. The world is seen as a bar after a while. The hours, the dulling, the deadening surroundings, the competition, the hassles, the drinking which produces maudlinism or aggressiveness of an ugly sort. It is no wonder that no one can sustain a high level of creativity without stimulants of some sort."

A few years ago he appeared with his group for a prolonged engagement at a Chinese restaurant on Fifty-second Street. Until he has conditions which suit him he will probably stay in his big studio home in Flushing, Long Island, with his family, his students, and a roomful of splendid recording equipment.

WHAT TO READ

Stein, Lou. "Lennie Tristano's 1st Album Heralds a New Genius." *Down Beat.* October 8, 1947. P. 18.

Tristano, Lennie. "What's Right with the Beboppers." *Metronome.* July 1947. Pp. 14, 31. Illus.

Tristano, Lennie. "What's Wrong with the Beboppers." *Metronome.* June 1947. P. 16, Illus.

Ulanov, Barry. "Master in the Making." *Metronome.* August 1949. Pp. 14–15, 32–33. Illus.

Ulanov, Barry. "The Means of Mastery." *Metronome.* September 1949. Illus.

Zeiger, Al. "Lennie Tristano, a Debt of Gratitude." *Metronome.* June 1955. Illus.

Cool and Quiet. Capitol T-371.

Lee Konitz with Tristano, Marsh, Bauer. Prestige 7004.

Line Up. Atlantic 1224.

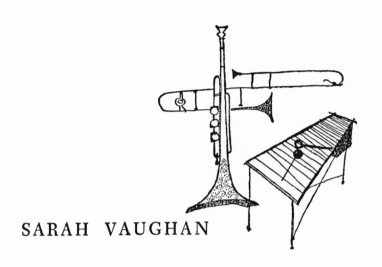

SARAH VAUGHAN

In August 1946, Sarah Vaughan and her
fiancé George Treadwell were on their way
home from Café Society Downtown, near
the West Fourth Street stop of the Sixth Avenue subway, when a gang of hoodlums beat them up.

Around 1951 she was approaching the big time
with *Down Beat, Esquire,* and *Metronome* awards.
Dave Garroway, a Chicago D.J., introduced her to
a Chicago theater audience: "Only once in each generation come a voice like this, one artist who brings
a new approach, a new way of communicating the
emotions which stir every soul."

The Divine One stepped out in the spotlight to
thrill the packed house. Her two-octave-range voice,
despite its drive, can break notes into eights, quarters,
and sixteenths along the way. Suddenly something
whizzed across the spotlight. Sassy put her hand to her

137

head in shocked surprise; red stains were on her white gown. Was she shot? she thought. No, race bigots were throwing ripe tomatoes. Garroway came out and said what he thought: "Yes, now you know. Now you have seen in capsule form the hate that pours poison into the heart of America. It started the last war, and even now, it's starting the next. Last night a bunch of hoodlums stormed the stage door, shouting, 'We'll show you you can't hire niggers.' Today they stop you from enjoying a great artist. Tomorrow, if you don't halt them, hate like this, magnified into war, will kill you and your children, too."

Sarah has been singing professionally since April 3, 1943. On that date she did exactly what Ella, her idol, had done, nine years before; she won an Apollo amateur contest. Coincidentally, Fitzgerald was the star attraction on the bill that night. Sarah was so nervous she forgot to kiss the "tree of hope" on the Apollo stage.

She was born in Newark, New Jersey, on March 27, 1924. One of her ambitions is to record an album of solo piano. She studied piano and organ from age seven to fifteen. She was vocalist and second pianist with the Earl Hines band in 1943.

The influences that shaped her musical thinking were all male: Parker, Gillespie, and Billy Eckstine. Her annual income is six-figured. She has two contracts with the same company, one for pops and the other for her first love, jazz.

138

She is partial to slacks and relaxes by reading comic books by the dozen. Of rehearsals: "I never have to rehearse, all I need is a group of good jazzmen."

WHAT TO READ

Feather, Leonard. "Sarah Vaughan." *Metronome.* July 1946. Pp. 21, 48–49.

"The Two-sided Sarah Vaughan." *Jazz Today.* June 1957. P. 11. Illus.

Ulanov, Barry. "The Human Sarah." *Metronome.* October 1949. Pp. 11–12. Illus.

Vaughan, Sarah. "Dark Girls Can Make It Too!" *Tan.* March 1953. Pp. 26–29, 46–48. Illus.

Vaughan, Sarah. Current Biography, 1957. Illus.

WHAT TO HEAR

After Hours.   Columbia CL-660.

In the Land of Hi-Fi.   Emarcy 36058.

My Kinda Love.   MGM 3274.

Sarah Vaughan.   Emarcy 36004.

Swingin' Easy.   Emarcy 36109.

LESTER YOUNG

Tenor-saxophonist Lester Young was the father of modern jazz, the quintessence of cool and the spiritual leader of the hip. One cannot have experienced jazz without listening to Pres.

He plays with tremendous drive, and yet in a relaxed manner. He has always avoided the lush, vibrato-filled tone, the drippy sentimental sax, in favor of a leaner sound. He departed from the short monotonous riff, making phrases long, breathy, and well constructed. He latches onto a note or two, suspends it, and the listener gets the feeling of suspension and then release as Pres jumps off into a swinging phrase.

Since 1936, when he came out with a revolutionary version of "Lady Be Good," he has never made a bad record. Some of the historic sides such as "Taxi War

Dance," "Shoeshine Boy," "Dickie's Dream," and "Twelfth Street Rag" were bootlegged by mysterious labels like Black Ace and peddled by record hustlers who for a dollar or so during the record ban could always put you on to a good thing. The influence of Pres led to a whole school of "Lester Young-type" tenormen, a few of which are Al Cohn, Zoot Sims, Allen Eager, Brew Moore, Stan Getz, and Ray Turner. There are many others.

Clellon Holmes in a short story entitled "The Horn" (later expanded to a novel) created a fictionalized portrait of Pres and a high mark in jazz literature: "Edgar Pool blew methodically, eyes beady and open, and he held his tenor saxophone horizontally extended from his mouth. This unusual posture gave it the look of some metallic albatross, caught insecurely in his two hands, struggling to resume flight." Pres said he held his horn at a 45-degree angle in order to avoid hitting the fellow in front of him in the early days of crowded K.C. bandstands and it became a habit.

Lester was meticulous yet sporty in dress, laconic in speech, and never ruffled or fazed by circumstance. Part of his philosophy (and the state of the American jazz artist) is illustrated in the following anecdote. Lester, playing somewhere in the Midwest, phoned a musician in New York to join him. The fellow was thrilled at the thought of playing with Young.

"How much does it pay?" he asked.

"Twenty-five cents." (Jazz talk for $25.)

142

"But, Pres," the musician said, "it costs $40 to get out there."

"Man," Lester answered, "you gotta save your money for these gigs."

On the morning of March 15, 1959, as Count Basie said, "We lost a precious jewel." It was a few hours after Pres returned from a trip to Paris. He knew he was dying and he wanted to die at home, in mid-Manhattan, the center of the world.

WHAT TO READ

Feather, Leonard. "Here's Pres." *The Melody Maker and Rhythm.* July 15, 1950. P. 3. Illus.

Harris, Pat. "Pres Talks about Himself, Copycats." *Down Beat.* May 4, 1949. P. 15.

Hentoff, Nat. "Lester Young." Shapiro, Nat, and Hentoff, Nat, *The Jazz Makers.* New York, Rinehart, 1957. Pp. 243–75. Discography. Illus.

Morrison, Allan. "You Got to Be Original, Man." *The Jazz Record.* July 1946. P. 7–9.

Reisner, Robert. "The Last, Sad Days of Lester Willis Young." *Down Beat.* April 30, 1959. P. 11.

Lester Leaps with Basie. Vol. 2. Jazz Panorama 1813.

Blue Lester. Savoy 12068.

Tenor Sax. Aladdin 801.

Tenor Sax. Aladdin 802.

Lester's Here. Verve 8161.

THE PARLANCE OF HIP

This Article Was First Published,
in somewhat shorter form,
in Esquire, November 1959

THE PARLANCE OF HIP

Jazz slang is continually changing. It changes because a term becomes distasteful to its originators as soon as it becomes too popular. One visit to a night club or the use of the word "man" and "dig" does not make one a cat. The language, like any other, has evolved, and its sole reason for existence is the fact that new words, or meanings, were needed to express specific attitudes. Lennie Tristano says, "Jazzmen come to grips with emotions so strong that they are unable to cope with them in ordinary adjectives. They are then gassed, fractured, killed, tore up. A wonderful instrumentalist is too much, the end, gone." The advertising world runs to an excessive use of superlatives: colossal, amazing, and so on. The modern jazzman has solved his own language problems by effecting the

147

reverse. A colossal performer is described as bad, terrible, a bitch, insane.

The language changes, too, in order to keep one step ahead of narcotics agents and other fuzz. Yet with the pattern of synonyms for drugs that runs throughout, not all or even many who use the language use the stuff.

The patterns of preoccupation are evident — music, women, cars, etc.

The entire vocabulary of hip consists of perhaps three hundred words and phrases, but one word can be used in many ways. A good example is the word "cool." Besides its adjectival and musical meaning, there are others. Following is an imaginary conversation between A, using King's English, and B, a Cool Cat.

A. I am moved to censure x strongly for stealing my fiancée.

B. Be cool, man. (In stopping a fight or cautioning a person against losing his temper or of the approach of the policeman, one can also say, "Cool it.")

A. You're right. I'll forget it . . . . Do you want to go to the movies?

B. It's cool with me (acquiescence).

A. Do you have enough money?

B. I'm cool (in good financial condition).

A. But aren't you supposed to play with that orchestra with which you have been rehearsing?

148

B. I'm cooling tonight (not playing).

A. Shall I call on x and take him with us?

B. I'm cooling on him (ignoring a person or subtly snubbing him).

A. You used to have a terrible addiction to ice cream. Shall we buy some at the next corner?

B. No, I'm cooling (tapering off).

A. Then you must be feeling lean and strong?

B. I'm cool (in good shape).

A. All right, let's go.

B. Cool.

The word "like" is a staple of the speech. It is used as a form of punctuation, or it may be used as a compliment, a ploy, and even as a substitution for completing a thought. (Example: Man, you know the story, like it's too much.) The speaker may deliberately leave something unsaid because he flatters your intuitive sense. He may also use "like" because he doesn't know, but thinks a "Man, like you dig," will cover him. The Beatniks are particularly prone to use this last device. (They have, incidentally, contributed almost nothing to the language. Lacking the fundamental intellectual honesty of the hipster, they are content to scrounge around after his semantic scraps.)

But above all, the hipster is, again, a cool creature — subtle, mocking, perverse, funny — and from attitudes spring most of the identifying characteristics of his speech. A primer follows.

149

A

ACE: buddy, good friend. Also dollar. Example: Lay
an ace on me till the weather breaks. Give me a
dollar until things get better.

ACTION: that which is happening. Example: Where's
the action (crap game)?

AX: instrument, horn. Extended to mean any tool
of work. Example: Hemingway's ax is his type-
writer.

B

BABY: a general appellation directed at either sex.

BAD: good. Example: A bad man on flute. A superla-
tive musician on flute.

BALL, BALLING: good time. Example: Let's have a
ball. Let's have a good time. Balling a chick.
Making love to a girl. *See also:* PARTY, TO.

BASH: a party.

BEAR: an unattractive girl.

BEAT: exhausted.

BEAT, TO: to swindle. Example: He beat me for my
bread.

BENNIES: Benzedrine pills.

BIFFER: an ugly girl. Example: I was out with a
biffer last night, which proves I dig distortion.

BITCH: something very good. Example: That tune
is a bitch. That song is beautiful. Bitch also

means girl or woman, but not in a derogatory sense. Example: I've got me a fine bitch.

BLAST, TO: to get high.

BLOOD: wine.

BLOW: to play. Example: Let's blow "Stardust." The word has been extended to anything spoken or performed. Example: He blows fine poetry.

BLOWIN' SNAKES: playing badly.

BOGUE: fake, false or bogus.

BOMB: an individual performance or occurrence that fails badly.

BOMBER: a large marijuana cigarette.

BOO: marijunana. Also, GAGE, GREENS, HEAD, MARY JANE, PIGFOOT, POT, SOUL, TEA, VONCE.

BOOT: a Negro man or woman.

BOX: phonograph, or piano, or guitar.

BOXED: to be in an encasing high. Stoned.

BREAD: money. Example: Is the bread cool? Is the salary or remuneration adequate?

BROOM: hat.

BUG TO: annoy or perturb. Example: This cat really bugs me. This person irritates me.

BUFFS: devotees.

BURN: cook.

BURN, TO: to rob.

BURNED: to be shot.

BUSTED: arrested.

C

C: cocaine. Also girl.

CANAL: bridge or change of tune.

CACK: fall asleep, fall out.

CAT: in the finest sense, a person who swings with life.

CENT: dollar. Example: This gig pays twenty cents a night. This job pays twenty dollars a night.

CHARGE: marijuana.

CHICK: girl.

CHIP: girl.

CHIPPIE: to dabble with narcotics; to take subcutaneous injections once in a while.

CHOPS: lips.

CLEAN: not to have any on one's person or free from the habit. Free from money.

COCKTAIL: to take a roach (see term) and fit it into a regular cigarette *so as to smoke it without burning your fingers.*

COINS: One asks for coins instead of a specific amount of small change.

COLD TURKEY: a narcotics cure in which the removal is sudden and complete rather than gradual diminution.

COME DOWN: wearing off of a high.

COMES ON: attitude, approach. Example: He comes on strong.

152

CONNECTION: one's source of supply.

COOK: to play well.

COOL: descriptive of a type of jazz. Also, a word of assent (*see* Introduction).

COOL ON: ignoring or snubbing. Example: I'm cooling on Jim. Also: to cool a cat is to make him aware of what is going on around him.

COOLING: unemployed.

COOLING IT: tapering off.

COP, TO COP: to obtain either by stealing or buying or permanent loan.

COP A PLEA: ask forgiveness, beg.

COP OUT: go to sleep. Evasiveness. Excuse.

CRAZY: assent, agreement. Adjective, wonderful.

CRIB: house, apartment.

CRUMBCRUSHER: baby.

CRUMBS: a small amount of money. Small bread (money).

CRUMBSNATCHER: child.

CUT, CUT OUT: (1) to depart. Example: Let's cut this pad. Let's leave this apartment. (2) to best. Example: Bud Powell could cut or chew up any pianist in sight.

CUT-BUDDY: Your closest friend, your ace.

D

DAD: a form of friendly or neutral address.

DAP: dapper. (Sharp is obsolete.)

DEALER: Pusher or drug vendor.

DICTY: snooty, stuck up.

DIG: to understand or comprehend. Also to listen. Example: Dig this gone book. Read this excellent tome.

DOG: unattractive girl.

DOG TUNE: poor piece of music.

DO UP, TO: term of action. Example: Let's go out and do up this club (enjoy it to the utmost.).

DOWN: dirty, earthy. Example: A down stud. A fellow devoid of pretense, fundamentally honest.

DOWN WITH SOMETHING, TO BE: to know something thoroughly.

DRAG: an annoying person.

DRAGGED: depressed. Example: I'm dragged with this scene. I'm annoyed by these surroundings.

DRIBBLE: to saunter, walk. Example: He dribbled down to her crib. He went to her apartment.

DRUGGED: annoyed, disgusted, extremely depressed.

DUGIE: heroin.

DYKE or BULL-DYKE: a lesbian.

E

END, THE: the best, the utmost.

ENDSVILLE: the greatest.

EYES: to want, to desire. Example: I have big eyes

154

to make it with this chick. I am very desirous of conquering this woman.

F

FACE: person, man.

FAG: a male homosexual.

FAGGOT JAZZ: flutey music with an effete beat.

FALL BY: to visit.

FALL IN: to enter.

FALL OUT: to leave, to sleep. Pass out from too much drugs.

FALL OUT LAUGHING, TO: to break up with mirth. Example: The cats fell out laughing.

FANGS: lips.

FAR OUT: very advanced; something intricate or involved, musically or otherwise. Jackson Pollock is far out.

FINGER-POPPER: a tune that makes you snap your fingers.

FIX: a shot of heroin or any other potent drug.

FLICK: a movie.

FLAKE: to sleep.

FLIP: noun, eccentric person; verb, to flip, means to go wild. Example: He flipped over the record. He waxed enthusiastic about the record. Obsolete: flipped his lid or flipped his wig. This has been shortened to just flipped. Flipped can also mean going insane.

FOXY: beautiful. Example: Man, but that's (she's) foxy!

FRACTURE: impress.

FRANTIC: (1) something of wild beauty. (2) Anything of a frenzied nature.

FREEBEE: something for nothing, a person who always looks for free things.

FUNKY: earthy. Originally meant an obnoxious smell, a repellent stench. It now refers to music with a basic, down home, hard beat.

FUZZ: police.

G

GAGE: marijuana. *See also:* POT, TEA, REEFER, JOINT, SOUL.

GAS: excite, overwhelm. Example: His act was a gas. His performance was great.

GASSER: a person or thing that brings forth tremendous enthusiasm.

GEETS: money.

GIG: job. He was gigging all over. He was playing different jobs all over the country.

GIRL: cocaine.

GITA: short for *Bhagavad-Gita,* a scripture of India with a religious attraction for jazz musicians.

GO: to act without inhibition.

GOIES: Dexedrine, Benzedrine.

GONE: very fine (nearly obsolete).

GOOD PEOPLE: a good person. Example: He's good people.

GOOF, TO: waste time. Example: Instead of working he was goofing off.

GORILLA: (1) violently drunk. (2) To gorilla someone means to strong-arm the person.

GRAY: a white person.

GREASE: food.

GREEN: marijuana.

GROOVE: category. A person's predilection. Example: Chess is his groove. He enjoys chess. Example: Not in my groove. Not in my category. To groove someone means to provide them with enjoyment. Example: Her singing grooved me.

GUN: horn.

H

HACKED: tired, irritated.

HAME: a position outside the music business.

HANDKERCHIEF HEAD: a Negro who toadies to whites.

HARD SHELLS: strong, addictive narcotics.

HASH: hashish.

HASSLE: heated discussion; squabble; trouble.

HAWK, THE: cold weather.

HEAD: old-time marijuana user. *See also* OLD HEAD.

HEAVY CREAM: a large, buxom woman.

HENCHMEN: friends.

HIGH: to be in a blissful, euphoric state induced by drugs, sex, alcohol, or any stimulant.

HIP: in the know, aware. Example: No need to tell me, I'm hip (meaning, I understand). Example: Don't be unhip. Don't be obtuse.

HIPPIE: a young person who is trying to put on hip airs, but doesn't quite make it.

HIPPY: refers to one who may be overly hip.

HIPSTER: one who is aware, as opposed to one who is square.

HIT ON, TO: (1) to request money. (2) Attempt seduction. Example: To hit on a chick means to try to become intimate with her.

HOLDING: to have marijuana on one's person.

HOOKED: to become an addict.

HORSE: heroin.

HUBCAP: important fellow.

HUMMER: a minor mistake, something that shouldn't have happened. Example: I got busted on a hummer.

158

HUNG UP: state of frustration, being in bad shape. Example: This cat really hung me up.

HUSTLE: to work at a job.

HUSTLER: prostitute, pimp, or number writer. One who makes his living illegally.

HYPE: deception. Example: He pulled a hype on the crowd. He fooled or cheated the crowd.

I

INSANE: very good.

J

JAZZ: categorical term meaning matter, stuff, or business (almost obsolete).

JIM: a form of unfriendly address, cold, as in, "Jim, don't bug me."

JIVE: to fool, to kid. The adjective is bogus.

JIVIN': fooling, jesting or teasing.

JOINT: marijuana cigarette.

JOLT: injection of narcotics.

JUG: a bottle of liquor.

JUICE: any form of liquor.

JUNKIE: a drug addict.

K

KICKS: pleasure.

KILL: delight.

KOOK: a crazy person. *See also:* CRAZY.

L

LAME, A: one who doesn't know what's happening, unsophisticated.

LATCH ON: to get with it.

LATER: word of departure, short for I'll see you later. Also means nothing doing. Example: Later for that.

LAY or LAY ON: to give something. Example: He laid ten cents on me. He gave me ten dollars.

LAY DEAD: to wait. To stay in one place, don't move.

LAY OUT: not to play. Example: A musician may tell another one to lay out on this chorus.

LAY UP: to be off the scene.

LID: hat (obsolete). *See also:* SKY.

LIFE, THE: the world of prostitution.

LIKE: a form of punctuation (*See* Introduction).

LOOSE WIG: one who is a very advanced performer.

M

MAKE IT, TO: success in any venture, big or small.

MAN: Most common form of address. Word used for emphasis.

MAN, THE: police. Also anyone in a position of authority.

MARY JANE: marijuana.

MATINEE: sexual intercourse in the afternoon.

MEAN: the best, greatest.

MEET: a jam session: Example: There's going to be a meet tonight.

MOLDY FIG: a term applied by lovers of modern jazz to a person partial to the older forms. Figs are usually interested in Chicago and New Orleans jazz.

MOM: the girl who takes the female role in a lesbian affair.

MOTHER JIVER: someone who cons or fools. Lately this has taken on affectionate meaning, even as a term of praise. Example: A bad mother jiver is an excellent musician.

MUSICIAN'S FREAK: a girl who bestows her favors only on musicians.

MY MAN: friend.

MY WOMAN: pimp's expression for a woman who would do anything for him.

N

NERVOUS: something that's so interesting it captures your attention. Example: That solo was real nervous.

NOTHIN'S HAPPENING: Specifically, no good musical ideas are forthcoming.

NOWHERE: the absolute of nothing. Example: That guy is nowhere.

NUTTY: great, exceptional.

O

O.D.: an overdose of narcotics.

OFAY: a white person. Sometimes shortened to fay
(derivation: pig Latin for foe).

OLD HEAD: a long-time user of marijuana.

OLD LADY: Wife or sweetheart; girl with whom one
sleeps.

ON THE NOD: sleeping, usually in a standing or sitting
position.

OUTLAW: a prostitute who does not have a pimp.

P

PAD: home or bed.

PARTY, TO: to have a good time. *See also:* TO BALL.

PARTYING: To continue on a long series of pleasures.
Example: I partied all that weekend.

PHONY DOWN: an insincere person.

PICK UP ON, TO: to obtain, to find; to understand,
appreciate.

PIC: phonograph.

PIECE: a gun.

PIERCING, TOO: overbearing.

PIGFOOT: obsolete expression for marijuana; also
muggles.

PIN, TO PIN: pin is to view or see something; to pin

162

is to point out, as a specimen. Example: The squares are trying to pin us, but like let's pin them.

POP: the girl who takes the male role in a lesbian affair.

POPPED: Caught (with drugs in one's possession). Example: I got popped.

POT: marijuana.

POUND: a five-dollar bill.

PUSH: verb, sell drugs; noun, a car. Example: You got a push? Do you have a car?

PUSHER: drug peddler.

PUT DOWN: to reject, to disparage.

PUT ON: to make fun of, or ridicule without the victim being aware of it.

R

RANCH: house.

RANK: stupid.

REEFER: marijuana (obsolete).

ROACH: the butt of a marijuana cigarette.

RUN OUTTA MY LIFE: stop bothering me. Example: Run outta my life and go play in the traffic.

S

SAGGIES: Seconals.

163

SALTY: angry. Example: Don't jump salty. Don't get angry.

SAYING SOMETHING: contributing something interesting in a musical solo or in any endeavor. Opposite would be, "Nothing happening."

SCARF: eat.

SCENE: a particular place or atmosphere. Example: I can't make this scene. I can't stand this situation.

SCOFF UP: to eat.

SCORE, TO: to attain success, to get what you want. Example: I scored with that chick.

SCUFFLE: to be down and out.

SET: a party.

SHADES: dark glasses.

SHAPE UP: getting one's affairs in order. To get certain things straight in order to do other things.

SHARP: fashionable (obsolete).

SHOE: a Negro man or woman. *See also:* BOOT.

SHORT: automobile.

SHUCK: a falsehood, deception, fraud. Example: Don't shuck me. Don't fool me.

SIAM: jail.

SKY: hat.

SLAM: jail

SMACK: heroin.

164

SMACKO: a drug addict. *See also:* JUNKIE.

SNAKE: the subway.

SNIFF: to inhale cocaine or heroin.

SOMETHING ELSE: so good that it is in a category all by itself.

SONNET: radio commercial.

SOUL: acme of sensitivity. Example: This cat has a lot of soul.

SOUND ON, TO: To ask someone for something. Example: I sounded on this stud about the bread. I spoke to this fellow about the money.

SPADE: a Negro.

SPIKE: a needle.

SPLIT: to leave. Example: Let's split. Let's leave.

SQUARE: unsophisticated. A person who lives solely by the book.

STACK, TO: to hide, to store.

STICK: a person's job or how he makes a living.

STING, THE: the price, admission.

STONE: adjective meaning complete. Example: He's a stone musician.

STONE: drunk or high.

STRAIGHT: in good shape.

STRAIGHT, A: an ordinary cigarette.

STRAIGHTEN SOMEONE: to give a person the real truth or genuine article.

165

STROLLER: car.

STRUGGLE: to dance.

STRUNG OUT: in bad physical condition.

STUD: man.

STUFF: drugs in general.

SWING: to have a good time, enjoy oneself.

SWINGING: (1) music characterized by a certain, propelling momentum; (2) getting one's kicks or pleasure from life.

T

TALK TRASH: light banter, persiflage.

TASTE: (1) a drink; (2) money. A portion of anything good.

TEA: marijuana.

TERRIBLE: wonderful. Example: He's a terrible man on alto.

THREADS: clothes. Example: He's wearing a fancy set of threads. He's wearing a good suit.

TICKY: stale, outmoded.

TIGHT: very friendly, close relationship. Example: Damon was tight with Pythias.

TOM or UNCLE TOM: a Negro who does not try to maintain his complete dignity before whites.

TOO MUCH: remarkable. Excruciating in its sublimity.

TORE UP: extremely distressed.

166

TORTURE EYES: southern tour.

TOUGH: great.

TRICK: a fellow who pays a prostitute for sex. A girl turns so many tricks per night.

TUBE: can be television, but usually telephone. Example: Use the tube. Call me up.

TURKEY: a fool. *See also:* SQUARE, A LAME.

TURN OUT, TO: to turn a chick out means to have a girl working for you.

TURN SOMEONE ON, TO: to get them high on drugs or pot. Expanded to mean: interest someone in music.

TWISTED: confused.

U

UNDAP: sloppily dressed.

V

VIBRATIONS: atmosphere. Quality or degree of empathy between people.

VILLE: suffix which can be added to any word to emphasize it.

VINES: clothes.

VIPER: a marijuana smoker.

VONCE, DO THE: make love.

VONCE: marijuana.

W

WAIL: perform with inspiration.

WALLS: a room; usually a poor, bare apartment.

WASTED: (1) in bad physical shape; (2) inflicted severe bodily harm on an individual.

WASTE SOMEONE, TO: to do a person bodily harm.

WAY OUT: intricate in nature, very advanced.

WEIRDO: a weird person, eccentric.

WHAT'S SHAKIN'?: What's happening?

WHEEL: motorcycle.

WHEELS: car.

WHIPPED: extremely tired.

WHO'S TAKIN' CARE OF BUSINESS?: What musicians are playing?

WIG: a person who is far out intellectually.

WIG, TO: to think, to play. Example: John wigged up this plan.

WILD: remarkable.

WING: to do something without preparation, innovate.

WOODSHED: practice.

WORK: sexual intercourse.

WORKS: the apparatus for administering drugs.

Y

YEN: agonized craving for stuff.

YOU GOT IT ALL: the response to "what's new?" when there is nothing new.

Z

ZONKED: one who is stoned, high, drunk.

ZOOT: exaggerated, ostentatious (obsolete).

168